ALSO BY AMERICA'S TEST KITCHEN

The Perfect Pie

Vegetables Illustrated

The Ultimate Burger

Spiced

The New Essentials Cookbook

Cook's Illustrated Revolutionary Recipes

Tasting Italy: A Culinary Journey

How to Braise Everything

How to Roast Everything

Dinner Illustrated

The Complete Diabetes Cookbook

The Complete Slow Cooker

The Complete Make-Ahead Cookbook

The Complete Mediterranean Cookbook

The Complete Vegetarian Cookbook

The Complete Cooking for Two Cookbook

Cooking at Home with Bridget and Julia

Just Add Sauce

Nutritious Delicious

What Good Cooks Know

Cook's Science

The Science of Good Cooking

The Perfect Cake

The Perfect Cookie

Bread Illustrated

Master of the Grill

Kitchen Smarts

Kitchen Hacks

100 Recipes: The Absolute Best Ways to Make the True Essentials

The New Family Cookbook

The America's Test Kitchen Cooking School Cookbook

The Cook's Illustrated Baking Book

The Cook's Illustrated Meat Book

The Cook's Illustrated Cookbook

The America's Test Kitchen Family Baking Book

The Best of America's Test Kitchen (2007–2020 Editions)

The Complete America's Test Kitchen TV Show Cookbook 2001–2019

Instant Pot® Ace Blender Cookbook

Air Fryer Perfection

Cook It in Your Dutch Oven

Sous Vide for Everybody

Multicooker Perfection

Food Processor Perfection

Pressure Cooker Perfection

Vegan for Everybody

Naturally Sweet

Foolproof Preserving

The How Can It Be Gluten-Free Cookbook

The How Can It Be Gluten-Free Cookbook: Volume 2

The Best Mexican Recipes

Slow Cooker Revolution

Slow Cooker Revolution Volume 2: The Easy-Prep Edition

The Six-Ingredient Solution

The America's Test Kitchen D.I.Y. Cookbook

THE COOK'S ILLUSTRATED ALL-TIME BEST SERIES

All-Time Best Brunch

All-Time Best Dinners for Two

All-Time Best Sunday Suppers

All-Time Best Holiday Entertaining

All-Time Best Appetizers

All-Time Best Soups

COOK'S COUNTRY TITLES

One-Pan Wonders

Cook It in Cast Iron

Cook's Country Eats Local

The Complete Cook's Country TV Show Cookbook

FOR A FULL LISTING OF ALL OUR BOOKS

CooksIllustrated.com

AmericasTestKitchen.com

PRAISE FOR AMERICA'S TEST KITCHEN TITLES

"This impressive installment from America's Test Kitchen equips readers with dozens of repertoire-worthy recipes. . . . This is a must-have for beginner cooks and more experienced ones who wish to sharpen their skills."
Publishers Weekly (starred review) on The New Essentials Cookbook

"A one-volume kitchen seminar, addressing in one smart chapter after another the sometimes surprising whys behind a cook's best practices. . . . You get the myth, the theory, the science, and the proof, all rigorously interrogated as only America's Test Kitchen can do."
NPR on The Science of Good Cooking

"The Perfect Cookie . . . is, in a word, perfect. This is an important and substantial cookbook. . . . If you love cookies, but have been a tad shy to bake on your own, all your fears will be dissipated. This is one book you can use for years with magnificently happy results."
The Huffington Post on The Perfect Cookie

Selected as one of the 10 Best New Cookbooks of 2017
The LA Times on The Perfect Cookie

Selected as the Cookbook Award Winner of 2017 in the Baking category
International Association of Culinary Professionals (IACP) on Bread Illustrated

Selected as one of Amazon's Best Books of 2015 in the Cookbooks and Food Writing category
Amazon on The Complete Vegetarian Cookbook

"This book upgrades slow cooking for discriminating, 21st-century palates—that is indeed revolutionary."
The Dallas Morning News on Slow Cooker Revolution

"Some 2,500 photos walk readers through 600 painstakingly tested recipes, leaving little room for error."
Associated Press on The America's Test Kitchen Cooking School Cookbook

"This book is a comprehensive, no-nonsense guide . . . a well-thought-out, clearly explained primer for every aspect of home baking."
The Wall Street Journal on The Cook's Illustrated Baking Book

"If there's room in the budget for one multicooker/Instant Pot cookbook, make it this one."
Booklist on Multicooker Perfection

"The book offers an impressive education for curious cake makers, new and experienced alike. A summation of 25 years of cake making at ATK, there are cakes for every taste."
The Wall Street Journal on The Perfect Cake

"Some books impress by the sheer audacity of their ambition. Backed up by the magazine's famed mission to test every recipe relentlessly until it is the best it can be, this nearly 900-page volume lands with an authoritative wallop."
Chicago Tribune on The Cook's Illustrated Cookbook

"The 21st-century Fannie Farmer Cookbook or The Joy of Cooking. If you had to have one cookbook and that's all you could have, this one would do it."
CBS San Francisco on The New Family Cookbook

"The go-to gift book for newlyweds, small families, or empty nesters."
Orlando Sentinel on The Complete Cooking for Two Cookbook

"The sum total of exhaustive experimentation . . . anyone interested in gluten-free cookery simply shouldn't be without it."
Nigella Lawson on The How Can It Be Gluten-Free Cookbook

"This encyclopedia of meat cookery would feel completely overwhelming if it weren't so meticulously organized and artfully designed. This is Cook's Illustrated at its finest."
The Kitchn on The Cook's Illustrated Meat Book

"It's all about technique and timing, and the ATK crew delivers their usual clear instructions to ensure success. . . . The thoughtful balance of practicality and imagination will inspire readers of all tastes and skill levels."
Publishers Weekly (starred review) on How to Roast Everything

HOW TO COCKTAIL

RECIPES AND TECHNIQUES FOR BUILDING THE BEST DRINKS

AMERICA'S TEST KITCHEN

Library of Congress Cataloging-in-Publication Data
Names: America's Test Kitchen (Firm), author.
Title: How to cocktail : recipes and techniques for building the best drinks / America's Test Kitchen.
Description: Boston, MA : America's Test Kitchen, [2019] | Includes bibliographical references and index.
Identifiers: LCCN 2019019257 (print) | ISBN 9781945256943 (hardcover)
Subjects: LCSH: Cocktails.
Classification: LCC TX951 .H687 2019 (print) | DDC 641.87/4--dc23
LC record available at
https://lccn.loc.gov/2019019257

AMERICA'S
TEST KITCHEN ®

AMERICA'S TEST KITCHEN
21 Drydock Avenue, Boston, MA 02210

Manufactured in the United States of America
10 9 8 7 6 5 4 3 2 1

Distributed by Penguin Random House Publisher Services

Tel: 800.733.3000

Pictured on front cover Manhattan (page 50)

Photography by Steve Klise

Featured Food Styling by Elle Simone Scott

Cocktail Advisor Nick Korn

Editorial Director, Books **Elizabeth Carduff**

Executive Editor **Adam Kowit**

Executive Food Editor **Dan Zuccarello**

Deputy Food Editor **Anne Wolf**

Senior Editors **Valerie Cimino, Joseph Gitter, Nicole Konstantinakos, Sara Mayer**

Associate Editors **Camila Chaparro, Lawman Johnson**

Editorial Assistant **Brenna Donovan**

Art Director, Books **Lindsey Timko Chandler**

Deputy Art Directors **Allison Boales, Courtney Lentz, Janet Taylor**

Associate Art Director **Katie Barranger**

Photography Director **Julie Bozzo Cote**

Photography Producer **Meredith Mulcahy**

Senior Staff Photographers **Steve Klise and Daniel J. van Ackere**

Staff Photographer **Kevin White**

Food Styling **Catrine Kelty, Chantal Lambeth, Elle Simone Scott**

Photoshoot Kitchen Team

Photo Team and Special Events Manager **Timothy McQuinn**

Lead Test Cook **Jessica Rudolph**

Assistant Test Cooks **Sarah Ewald, Hannah Fenton, Jacqueline Gochenouer, Eric Haessler**

Senior Manager, Publishing Operations **Taylor Argenzio**

Production Manager **Christine Spanger**

Imaging Manager **Lauren Robbins**

Production and Imaging Specialists **Dennis Noble, Jessica Voas, Amanda Yong**

Copy Editor **Jeffrey Schier**

Proofreader **Ann-Marie Imbornoni**

Indexer **Elizabeth Parson**

Chief Creative Officer **Jack Bishop**

Executive Editorial Directors **Julia Collin Davison and Bridget Lancaster**

CONTENTS

WELCOME TO AMERICA'S TEST KITCHEN

This book has been tested, written, and edited by the folks at America's Test Kitchen. Located in Boston's Seaport District in the historic Innovation and Design Building, it features 15,000 square feet of kitchen space, including multiple photography and video studios. It is the home of *Cook's Illustrated* magazine and *Cook's Country* magazine and is the workday destination for more than 60 test cooks, editors, and cookware specialists. Our mission is to test recipes over and over again until we understand how and why they work and until we arrive at the best version.

We start the process of testing a recipe with a complete lack of preconceptions, which means that we accept no claim, no technique, and no recipe at face value. We simply assemble as many variations as possible, test a half-dozen of the most promising, and taste the results blind. We then construct our own recipe and continue to test it, varying ingredients, techniques, and cooking times until we reach a consensus. As we like to say in the test kitchen, "We make the mistakes so you don't have to." The result, we hope, is the best version of a particular recipe, but we realize that only you can be the final judge of our success (or failure). We use the same rigorous approach when we test equipment and taste ingredients.

All of this would not be possible without a belief that good cooking, much like good music, is based on a foundation of objective technique. Some people like spicy foods and others don't, but there is a right way to sauté, there is a best way to cook a pot roast, and there are measurable scientific principles involved in producing perfectly beaten, stable egg whites. Our ultimate goal is to investigate the fundamental principles of cooking to give you the techniques, tools, and ingredients you need to become a better cook. It is as simple as that.

To see what goes on behind the scenes at America's Test Kitchen, check out our social media channels for kitchen snapshots, exclusive content, video tips, and much more. You can watch us work (in our actual test kitchen) by tuning in to *America's Test Kitchen* or *Cook's Country* on public television or on our websites. Download our award-winning podcast *Proof*, which goes beyond recipes to solve food mysteries (AmericasTestKitchen.com/proof), or listen in to test kitchen experts on public radio (SplendidTable.org) to hear insights that illuminate the truth about real home cooking. Want to hone your cooking skills or finally learn how to bake—with an America's Test Kitchen test cook? Enroll in one of our online cooking classes. And you can engage the next generation of home cooks with kid-tested recipes from America's Test Kitchen Kids.

However you choose to visit us, we welcome you into our kitchen, where you can stand by our side as we test our way to the best recipes in America.

facebook.com/AmericasTestKitchen
twitter.com/TestKitchen
youtube.com/AmericasTestKitchen
instagram.com/TestKitchen
pinterest.com/TestKitchen

AmericasTestKitchen.com
CooksIllustrated.com
CooksCountry.com
OnlineCookingSchool.com
AmericasTestKitchen.com/kids

IN THE COCKTAIL KITCHEN

AN INTRODUCTION

You are holding in your hands the first-ever cocktail book from America's Test Kitchen. You may be asking yourself, What took so long? Well, after we finished creating this book, we found ourselves asking the very same question!

Just like cooking, cocktail making is part art and part science. And as with cooking, you may prefer your cocktails sweeter, or less sweet, or with more lemon juice (or with more whiskey). But regardless of personal flavor preferences, there remains a best-practices approach to using specific techniques when making cocktails to produce the most delicious, consistent results every time. It's that kitchen tested and kitchen-perfected approach that we have brought to bear, navigating our subject from the perspective of a home cook rather than from that of an amateur "mixologist" (a term we have purposefully avoided using).

Each chapter illustrates a fundamental technique of cocktail making, from simply building a drink directly in the serving glass to using a shaker correctly to muddling herbs and fruit to extract their flavors. We've also included two DIY chapters, which resulted from our realization of how expensive (and full of additives)

liqueurs and vermouths can be and how easy, satisfying, and creative it is to make your own.

Along the way, we did side-by-side tastings of bourbons, ryes, rums, orange liqueurs, anise liqueurs, vermouths, tonic waters, and more to figure out which ones might be acceptable substitutes for each other. We created spreadsheets to measure the amount of bitters that come out of a bottle in a drop versus a dash, and out of a half-full bottle versus a full bottle, even taking into account the size of the bottles and the apertures. We made dozens of batches of ice using tap, filtered, and distilled water, freezing it in multiple ways and in multiple sizes, to develop our recipe for Practically Clear Ice (page 224).

We always kept the home cook in mind, solving practical challenges like how to make an array of cocktails without having to purchase lots of expensive bottles, what tools you really need (and how to wield them like a pro), how to make big batches for entertaining, and so much more.

We hope you have as much fun in your kitchen mixing up these cocktails as we did creating them in our test kitchen. Cheers!

TOP TIPS FOR TRANSCENDENT COCKTAILS

IT'S ALL ABOUT TECHNIQUE.
We feel so strongly about this principle that we organized this entire book around it. Cocktail technique is not difficult, so it's easy to lull yourself into thinking that it's not important. But following our instructions for how to and how long to stir, shake, muddle, garnish, and more will deliver consistently impressive, tantalizingly delicious results every time.

HIGHER-QUALITY INGREDIENTS MAKE HIGHER-QUALITY COCKTAILS.
Even though you are mixing spirits and liqueurs in cocktails rather than consuming them on their own, quality still matters, so purchase the best you can afford. We're not suggesting you buy a $100 bottle of single-malt Scotch to make the Highlander (page 88), but the lowest-end bottle from the bottom shelf is probably not going to make a great cocktail. We tested and developed all of the cocktails in this book using bottles priced squarely in the middle price range. Chambord is a wonderful berry-flavored liqueur, but it's not inexpensive. If you love that flavor, turn to page 231 for our homemade Fruits of the Forest Liqueur. In fact, making some of your own liqueurs and mixers gives you excellent quality control as well as cost savings. Tasters preferred our homemade Sweet Vermouth (page 244) and Dry Vermouth (page 242) to any store-bought version. In general, we don't recommend brands in this book because we learned that this is a matter of (sometimes strong!) personal preference.

UNDERSTAND YOUR INGREDIENTS.
Spirits can be confusing. We've demystified the essentials for you, but given that the liquor store presents a vast world of choices, we recommend reading labels, doing some independent research, and not hesitating to talk with merchants about what kind of flavors you like and what level of quality you can get for what you're willing or able to spend.

WATER IS AN INGREDIENT.
There are only a few recipes where it actually appears on an ingredient list, but water and its diluting effects are critical to nuanced, well-balanced cocktails. Typically water is incorporated into cocktails by shaking or stirring the ingredients along with ice. Additionally, some cocktails are then served on the rocks. In testing, we found that it was well worth the effort to pay attention to both the quality of water used to make cocktail ice and the technique of making the ice. See page 224 for more on how to make Practically Clear Ice.

CHILL YOUR GLASSES IN THE FREEZER.
As mentioned, usually the water in a cocktail comes from melted ice, with the goal of the ice being to chill your drink as well as dilute it correctly. Chilling your serving glasses, which takes only a few minutes, ensures that all that frosty goodness you've created in the cocktail shaker or mixing glass won't be lost by pouring your carefully made cocktail into a room-temperature glass.

DOUBLE-STRAIN YOUR COCKTAILS (SOMETIMES).

It may seem fussy, but it's not. Whether a cocktail is shaken or stirred, it must be strained through either a built-in strainer (for a cobbler shaker) or a handheld strainer (for a Boston shaker). There are two situations when we recommend pouring your drink through a second, small conical strainer set over the serving glass. The first is for shaken cocktails served straight up (without ice); double-straining results in beautifully translucent cocktails with no floating ice shards. (An exception is straight-up cocktails containing egg whites, such as the Whiskey Sour, page 104, since double-straining deflates the desirable frothy foam that comes from shaking the egg white.) The other situation when we double-strain is for muddled cocktails; nobody wants to end up chewing on chunks of mint while trying to enjoy a Mojito (page 124).

ALWAYS MEASURE. NEVER EYEBALL.

For cocktails with a perfect balance of flavors every time, measure your ingredients. As little as ¼-ounce difference in lemon juice or Simple Syrup (page 198), for example, can make a significant difference in the outcome of your drink. This tip includes bitters! Traditionally in cocktail recipes, bitters are called for in imprecise "dashes" or "drops." However, we learned in testing that the actual amount in a dash or drop can vary wildly depending on the diameter of the dropper, the size of the dasher, how much liquid is in the bottle, the size of the bottle, and even the force with which you wield the bottle. It's easy and consistent to drop or dash your bitters into a teaspoon measure before adding them to your cocktail. That's what we did, and that's what we recommend you do, too.

MEASURE IN OUNCES, NOT CUPS.

When cooking, we are all accustomed to measuring liquids in cup measures. However, greater precision is required for measuring the smaller amounts of liquids needed for cocktails. For the most consistent results, we developed our recipes using ounce measurements for liquid ingredients. Cocktail jiggers make it easy to measure this way. Think of cocktail making as similar to baking: Just as weighing the ingredients used in baking recipes provides more precise measurements and results in better baked goods, measuring liquids in ounces results in well-made, balanced cocktails every time. (We do use teaspoon measurements for amounts less than ¼ ounce.)

THE GARNISH IS NOT AN AFTERTHOUGHT.

Garnishes do more than look pretty; they add a significant flavor and aroma component that properly completes your carefully made drink. We tested all of our recipes both with and without garnishes, making adjustments until each drink had the optimal garnish. Flavored rim salts and sugars, homemade cocktail cherries and cocktail onions, and instructions for making and using citrus twists and peels can all be found in Chapter 7.

CONSIDER THE NONALCOHOLIC COCKTAIL.

Calling them "mocktails" does them a disservice. Spirit-free cocktails should be as attractive, thoughtfully balanced, and indulgent as any carefully crafted alcoholic cocktail. We developed our original nonalcoholic cocktail recipes as meticulously as we did our spirited cocktails, with the hope that they become part of your regular cocktail rotation. For a list of spirit-free cocktails, see page 13.

MESSAGE IN A BOTTLE

There are hundreds of different kinds of alcohol on store shelves. Here we explain the fundamental categories of spirits and liqueurs and make recommendations based on what we consider essential versus optional in order to have a versatile home bar. You can of course purchase additional bottles depending on what you like to drink, what flavors you enjoy, how much room you have in your bar cabinet, and how much money you are willing to spend.

THE SPIRIT WORLD

The most common types of base spirits are gin, vodka, whiskey, rum, tequila, and brandy. If you are able to stock one bottle of each at home, that will offer you the broadest cocktail options. Or choose the two or three that you enjoy the most, and work with those.

GIN

Gin starts as a neutral base spirit (often distilled from various grains), which is imbued with botanicals, most notably juniper (which gives gin that "piney" flavor). We developed our recipes using London dry gin, the standard-bearer of modern gin, which has an extremely versatile juniper-citrus flavor profile. That's what we recommend for a basic home bar, but if you love gin you might also try other styles, which include but are not limited to Plymouth gin (earthier and less dry than London dry and currently made by only one distillery), Old Tom (sweeter and less herbal than London dry), and Navy Strength (similar to London dry but with a higher alcohol content).

VODKA

The most neutral-tasting spirit, and probably the most versatile because of that neutrality, vodka in some form was made in Russia way back in the 14th century. It was traditionally distilled from potatoes, although in modern times it's more likely to be distilled from various grains, like wheat. It can even be made from fruits, like apples or grapes. Vodka is often overlooked in the modern bar because of its neutral flavor, but we love it in our Bichon Frise (page 114). It can also balance and temper other, stronger flavors, as it does with the tea liqueur in our Teatini (page 71).

WHISKEY

The world of whiskey is wide, with countries as divergent as Canada and Japan producing excellent whiskeys. All whiskey is made from grain, but different rules apply depending on the type of whiskey, and many factors affect their flavor profiles. In developing our recipes, we used primarily American whiskey, with a few exceptions (such as the Highlander, page 88, and Irish Coffee, page 43). We recommend having a bottle of both bourbon and rye in your liquor cabinet, if possible. Additional bottles beyond those are up to your personal preference.

American Whiskey

Bourbon is the quintessential American whiskey. It must be made from at least 51 percent corn and be aged in new charred oak barrels. It must be made in the United States (but not necessarily in Kentucky). The corn contributes a certain sweetness and round, full body to the whiskey. We prefer it in our Old-Fashioned (page 55).

While Tennessee whiskey has the same legal requirements as bourbon for raw materials and aging, it must be produced in Tennessee, and it is filtered through charcoal prior to aging. This extra filtering removes some of the stronger flavor compounds, resulting in a lighter-bodied, smoother-tasting whiskey. It's often a good substitute for bourbon, as in our Old-Fashioned (page 55), or for rye, as in our Manhattan (page 50).

Rye, which has many of the same legal production and aging requirements as bourbon, must be made from 51 percent rye. This results in a drier, spicier flavor and a slightly lighter body than the corn-heavy bourbon. We think it's ideal in cocktails that have a sweeter element, such as the Fancy Free (page 56), which has maraschino liqueur.

Other Whisk(e)y

Scotch has strict production and aging requirements. It must be made in Scotland and aged in oak barrels (often used bourbon barrels are employed to age Scotch). Many Scotches are made from malted barley, though other grains can be used. There are many terms used in relation to Scotch, each of which comes with specific requirements. The majority of Scotch is blended, and that's what we recommend for making cocktails. Depending on which you use, Scotch may bring a smoky or peaty note to cocktails.

Irish whiskey was the most popular spirit in the world during the 19th century. In fact, the word "whiskey" is derived from the Gaelic phrase *uisce beatha*, meaning "water of life." Irish whiskeys are generally made from malted barley or other grains, and they generally have less smoky or peaty flavors and aromas than Scotch. In our opinion, Irish whiskey is a must in Irish Coffee (page 43).

Canadian whisky can be made from corn, wheat, or rye. (Confusingly, it's allowed to be called "rye whisky" even if it doesn't include any rye.) Canadian whisky often offers great quality for a lower price than that of other whiskies.

Japanese whisky has a style that is strongly influenced by Scotch, but it tends to have a silkier, smoother texture. Also like Scotch, it tends to command high prices.

RUM

Rum is one of the more complicated spirits to understand, because it's so diverse and lacks the consistent production and labeling regulations that govern many other spirits. Rum can legally be made anywhere in the world, and the rules for making it vary accordingly. It's been produced in America since the 1600s. The one thing all rums have in common is that they are made from sugarcane and its products—more specifically, in most cases molasses.

Traditional classifications based on geography or color can be misleading: Raw materials can come from multiple locations, and regional styles and production methods have evolved over time. While most rum is aged to some degree, gaining complexity, a darker rum does not necessarily mean an older (or better) rum, because in some countries the color can come from additives (including sugar and caramel coloring) or filtering methods. White rums (sometimes called silver) may simply have been filtered to remove any color. More recent rum categorizations are attempting to clear up this confusion by classifying rums according to what they are made from, their production method, and their aging time.

For our cocktails, we found that we could rely primarily on two types: a white rum (an unaged or lightly aged—1 to 4 years—rum that may have been filtered) and an aged rum (a rum aged anywhere from 5 to 14 years). The lighter-bodied style of white rum was ideal for daiquiris and mojitos, while tiki drinks, in particular, benefited from the more complex, full-bodied flavors of aged rum. For our Dark and Stormy (page 29), we particularly liked the burnt-sugar flavors of Gosling's Black Seal Rum, though you could use aged rum. Be aware that rum, unlike other spirits in this section, can have sugar added to it before bottling, and this can affect the balance of flavors in your cocktails.

Cachaça
The national spirit of Brazil, where by law it is made exclusively, cachaça could be considered a type of rum. It differs in that it is made directly from fermented sugarcane juice rather than molasses, so it's a bit more floral, grassy, and herbaceous.

TEQUILA
By law, tequila must be produced in Mexico, from the blue agave plant (which is not a cactus). It can be bottled young (blanco) or be aged for up to 1 year (reposado) or 1 to 3 years or longer (añejo or extra añejo). We found that blanco and reposado are often interchangeable in cocktails, so you can purchase whichever one you prefer. Blanco tequila will generally give a cocktail a brighter, cleaner flavor, whereas reposado tequila will bring more nuanced, oaky notes to your drink. If you enjoy tequila, you might also like mezcal, which is made from various agave plants that are roasted, often adding a smoky component to its flavor profile.

BRANDY
Brandy is essentially distilled wine, of which cognac, made in the Cognac region of France, is considered the apex. But "distilled wine" doesn't have to mean grape wine; it can mean any fruit. For example, Calvados and applejack are both types of brandy made from apples. The cocktails in this book use cognac-style brandy unless otherwise specified.

MIX IT UP

Hundreds of liqueurs act as supplemental players, even major players, in the cocktail kitchen. No matter what flavor you like, you can find a liqueur to match, from hazelnuts to bananas to—yes—smoked salmon. We consider orange liqueur and sweet and dry vermouth to be essentials; the other liqueurs here will greatly expand your options.

ORANGE LIQUEUR

Orange liqueur is a fundamental building block of countless cocktails, including the Margarita (pages 152 and 170), the Sidecar (page 83), and the Corpse Reviver No. 2 (page 93). But if you've found yourself stumped by which orange liqueur to buy, you're not alone: These sweetened orange-flavored alcohols go by different names (many of which aren't legally protected) and can have different spirit bases, alcoholic strengths, and sweetness levels. Curaçao was historically a brandy- or rum- based orange liqueur made from bitter oranges grown on the Caribbean island of the same name. Nowadays, neutral spirits are also used, colors can be added, and curaçao can come from anywhere. Triple sec was originally an orange liqueur of French origin, made from a neutral-flavored clear spirit. Cointreau is one of the most famous and readily available brands of triple sec. Grand Marnier, another well-known brand of orange liqueur, is often called a curaçao-style orange liqueur, due to its cognac base.

While one may assume that any orange liqueur in a cocktail will do, which orange liqueur you use can make a difference in the cocktail's overall profile. If you're going to buy just one bottle, we suggest Cointreau or a similar high-quality triple sec. This style generally makes for a brighter, cleaner orange flavor in cocktails, particularly those using "lighter" spirits (like gin, tequila, or vodka). Just be aware that there is a wide range of alcohol content, sweetness, and flavor profiles across brands of triple sec. If you are able to buy a second type of orange liqueur, also try a brandy-based version, like Grand Marnier, which complements drinks that have deeper flavors or use darker spirits, like the Sidecar. Or better yet, you can make your own Orange Liqueur (page 228)!

OTHER FRUIT LIQUEURS

Maraschino liqueur plays a key role in many cocktails, including the Aviation (page 113) and the Fancy Free (page 56). Traditionally made from Marasca cherries, it is considered a dry rather than a sweet liqueur.

Berry liqueurs, like Chambord and crème de cassis, are great in punches or mixed with sparkling wine. Try our Fruits of the Forest Liqueur (page 231) in the Holiday Punch (page 189) or the Royal Berry (page 36).

Limoncello (page 232), made from lots of lemon zest, makes a martini-style Limontini (page 110) and is also perfect for solo sipping.

Chile liqueur is an up-and-comer for Southwestern-style drinks like the Tumbleweed (page 117). Our versatile Ancho Chile Liqueur (page 235) can be customized by using tequila, vodka, or bourbon as the base spirit (and by using different chiles instead of the ancho).

HERBAL LIQUEURS

Benedictine and Chartreuse are examples of sweeter-style herbal liqueurs, while Italian *amari* (a broad category) are often more lightly sweet or bittersweet (or even just plain bitter). These herbal liqueurs are frequently consumed on their own, after a meal, but they are increasingly making their way into cocktails. The Alcachofa (page 69) and the Fernet Fizz (page 109) are two of our favorites.

Anise liqueur is another herbal liqueur that plays a small but important role in cocktails, most notably the Sazerac (page 60). The most famous—or infamous—version is absinthe, which is potent and delicious, but expensive. In our testing, we found that Herbsaint

(originally made as an absinthe substitute), a dry pastis (such as Ricard), or an anisette labeled dry made an excellent alternative.

OTHER LIQUEURS

Amaretto is typically made from the bitter kernels found inside stone fruit pits (though some brands contain almonds). It has an almondy flavor profile, and it's worth buying for the Amaretto Sour (page 104) alone.

Floral liqueurs are most often associated with the elderflower-infused St-Germain, but you can also use lavender, chamomile, or jasmine flowers or rose petals (see page 236).

Coffee and tea liqueurs aren't just for dessert drinks. Make a sophisticated, not-too-sweet Espresso Martini with our Coffee Liqueur (page 241). Tea Liqueur (page 238) can be made from any type of tea and is used in the Teatini (page 71) and the Hole in One (page 135).

VERMOUTH

Vermouth is a type of fortified wine that is made from a base of white wine that is infused with a mixture of botanicals and then fortified with a neutral spirit (usually grain or grape alcohol) to raise its alcohol level. What traditionally distinguishes vermouth from other aromatized wines (like Lillet) is the inclusion of an herb called wormwood (from which the word "vermouth" is derived). Although there are many varieties, the two main ones are called "dry" and "sweet." Dry vermouths (also called white or French vermouth) have a more herbal flavor profile. Sweet vermouths (also called red or Italian vermouth) tend to have more floral and spiced flavors in addition to herbs. For longer shelf life, refrigerate your vermouth after opening.

IN THE LIMELIGHT

Nonalcoholic cocktail components are every bit as important to high-quality cocktails as the spirits and liqueurs you use. Here's a breakdown of our favorite home-bar essentials.

CITRUS

Citrus fruit is critical to cocktail making. The juice is one of the most common nonalcoholic mixers, and the peel is frequently used for garnishing. Our single-most important piece of advice regarding citrus is to always use fresh fruit—never juice from a bottle or carton. It's easy enough to squeeze citrus for one or two cocktails, but what if you're making big-batch cocktails? Do they suffer in quality if you squeeze ahead of time? The short answer is no. Lemon and lime juices can be squeezed a few hours ahead with no problem; in fact, some tasters felt they even improved in flavor. We do recommend squeezing oranges right before you plan to use them, since they contain a compound that turns bitter when exposed to air. Generally, one large lemon yields about 2½ ounces juice; one large lime yields about 1½ ounces juice; and one large orange yields about 3 ounces juice.

SIMPLE AND FLAVORED SYRUPS

Simple Syrup (page 198) refers to a 1-to-1 mixture of sugar and water. It is an essential ingredient in cocktails. Any other type of sugar syrup can be referred to as a flavored syrup, and your options are many. We developed versatile recipes for flavored syrups using fresh herbs and citrus fruits, as well as a Spiced Syrup using cinnamon, cloves, and allspice (see pages 198–199). We also created a tongue-tingling Ginger Syrup (page 208) that can be used in combination with seltzer for a customizable ginger beer.

Grenadine is a flavored syrup made using pomegranate juice, though many commercial brands use artificial flavor. Our Grenadine (page 201) is made from natural ingredients and adds its sweet yet tart flavor and ruby color to the Ombré Sling (page 103) and the Frozen Hurricane (page 159).

Orgeat is a syrup traditionally made from almonds and frequently flavored with orange blossom water. It is indispensable to tiki cocktails, including the Mai Tai (page 97) and Scorpion Cup (page 98). Store-bought versions can be toothachingly sweet and taste overwhelmingly of artificial almond extract. Our DIY Orgeat Syrup (page 202) is made from toasted blanched almonds and has a clean, natural almond flavor.

Shrub syrups are sweetened fruit-and-vinegar syrups that are frequently used in cocktails (see the Tartbreaker on page 94). They also make great nonalcoholic cocktails when mixed with seltzer. Our Mixed Berry, Peach, and Cranberry Shrub Syrups (pages 204–205) are great for keeping on hand in the refrigerator.

FIZZY WATERS

Seltzer is simply carbonated water, with no added ingredients. It's indispensable in cocktail making, particularly for highball-style cocktails that are built right in the glass, including our Favorite Gin and Tonic (page 22) and the Americano (page 30). It also is frequently used in nonalcoholic cocktails, as in our Grapefruit-Rosemary Spritzer (page 38).

Club soda is slightly different in that it has added minerals, which do affect its flavor. But it can be used as a substitution for seltzer.

Likewise, sparkling mineral water may be used for cocktails, but it is often less carbonated than seltzer, and since it commands a higher price as well, it's really not worth it.

Tonic water is essential for our Favorite Gin and Tonic (page 22). Commercial brands vary quite a bit in their levels of sweetness, bitterness, and quality. We developed a balanced Tonic Syrup (page 207) with bright citrus notes that we love to use in combination with seltzer in our two G&Ts (pages 22 and 66) and in the Lillet Tonique (page 25).

THE BITTER END

One ingredient that makes a huge impact in tiny amounts is cocktail bitters. But what are bitters, exactly? Behind the modern cocktail bar, bitters can be found in two main forms: potable bitters and nonpotable bitters. Potable bitters are liqueurs intended for sipping, usually as a digestif. This broad category includes Campari, Italian amari, and herb-based liqueurs like Jägermeister. What most people think of as cocktail bitters are the type called nonpotable bitters. These are not meant for sipping; rather, these intensely concentrated elixirs are designed to be added to cocktails in minuscule amounts, to add nuanced yet complex flavors and aromas.

There are hundreds of types of cocktail bitters. Some have a particular ingredient as their predominant flavor profile, like orange, mint, or maple bitters, and others are blends of many flavors, like Angostura bitters, certainly the most famous and well used of cocktail bitters. Stock a few different types and your seasoning options will increase exponentially. We developed recipes for three different bitters that will be the most versatile in your cocktail making. Old-Fashioned Aromatic Bitters (page 210) have a flavor profile in the style of Angostura bitters. Our Citrus Bitters (page 212) can be used anywhere orange or lemon bitters are called for. And our Cherry-Fennel Bitters (213) are somewhat reminiscent of Peychaud's bitters, the classic New Orleans bitters used in the Sazerac (page 60). We also suggest using our Cherry-Fennel Bitters wherever you might use cherry bitters, such as in whiskey-based cocktails.

To get the most out of your bitters, we recommend measuring them by the teaspoon (see page 16 for more information).

HELPFUL COCKTAIL LISTS

ONE-BOTTLE COCKTAILS

Gin

Favorite Gin and Tonic (page 22)
New-Fashioned Gin and Tonic (page 66)
Southside (page 91)
Ramos Gin Fizz (page 107)
Celery Gimlet (page 130)

Vodka

Moscow Mule (page 26)
Vodka Negroni (page 59)
Arugula Gimlet (page 130)
Bloody Marys for a Crowd (page 173)

Rum

Dark and Stormy (page 29)
Caribbean Coffee (page 43)
Daiquiri (page 80)
Piña Coladas (page 151)
Frozen Hurricanes (page 159)
Horchata Borracha (page 161)
Mojito (page 124)
House Punch (page 185)
Eggnog (page 190)

Whiskey

Irish Coffee (page 43)
Scotch Hot Toddy (page 44)
Old-Fashioned (page 55)
Whiskey Sour (page 104)
Bourbon-Cherry Slush (page 148)
Autumn in New England (page 133)
Mint Julep (page 144)
Rye-Basil Julep (page 144)
Whiskey-Ginger Smash (page 144)

Brandy

Hot Toddy (page 44)
Fireside (page 63)
Brandied Caramel Apple
Milkshakes (page 165)
Brandied Mulled Cider (page 192)

Tequila

Tartbreaker (page 94)

Cachaça

Caipirinha (page 127)

Amaretto

Amaretto Sour (page 104)
Chocolate-Amaretto Milkshakes (page 166)

Lillet

Lillet Tonique (page 25)

Pimm's No.1

Pimm's Cups (page 179)

Wine

Peach-Strawberry Frosé (page 156)
Peach Friesling (page 156)

Beer

Michelada (page 34)

BEHIND THE BAR

A sturdy cocktail shaker, a mixing glass and bar spoon, and a few strainers are essential pieces of home-bar equipment. There are two main types of cocktail shakers; the one you choose ultimately comes down to personal preference. Cobbler shakers come in a multitude of sizes, but our preferred size is about 24 ounces. For information on how to use a cobbler shaker, see page 84. For how to use a Boston shaker, see page 86. For how to stir using a mixing glass and bar spoon, see page 52. For measuring and cutting tools, turn the page.

COBBLER SHAKER

The most common choice for home bartenders, this is an easy-to-use three-piece shaker with a bottom mixing cup, a built-in strainer on top, and a cap to seal it. Metal and plastic components will be less likely than glass to break. Our winner, the Tovolo Stainless Steel 4-in-1, has a built-in citrus juicer on top.

BOSTON SHAKER

The choice of bartenders everywhere, this is what we used to develop our recipes. It consists of a bottom stainless steel cup and a top cup that looks like a pint glass but is made of tempered (safety) glass. The glass allows you to see your ingredients as you add them, which bartenders prefer to help prevent error. Our winner is the Boston Shaker Professional Boston Shaker.

MIXING GLASS

A straight-sided glass with a pouring spout is our choice for stirring cocktails over ice. Since glass is a better insulator than metal, a glass mixing glass will chill your cocktail more thoroughly.

BAR SPOON

A long twizzle-handled stainless steel bar spoon is essential to achieve maximum chilling with minimal dilution when stirring drinks with ice. For further information on stirring technique, see page 52.

JULEP STRAINER

This strainer predates the Hawthorne strainer and was developed for mint julep imbibers to hold over their cups to keep from getting a face full of crushed ice and mint. It fits well into a mixing glass, so we use it for stirred cocktails.

HAWTHORNE STRAINER

This strainer is made of a flat circular piece of metal with holes, bordered by a flexible spring. It fits neatly into a Boston shaker to catch ice and other solids. Look for one with a tight spring, which will catch smaller pieces of ice and solids and will make for a better-strained cocktail.

CONICAL STRAINER

We double-strain cocktails into the glass using a fine-mesh conical strainer. This provides further insurance against solid ingredients ending up in your glass and also prevents errant ice shards from diluting your cocktail. We make an exception for cocktails containing egg whites; you'll get more foam on top if you single-strain.

BEHIND THE BAR

MALLET AND LEWIS BAG
Putting ice for drinks like the Mai Tai (page 97) in a canvas bag and whacking it with a wooden mallet produces fluffier, drier crushed ice than if using a food processor. Plus, it's more fun.

ICE CUBE TRAYS
We recommend 1-inch silicone or rubber ice cube trays to make ice for shaking cocktails and 2-inch trays to make ice for serving. Our favorite 2-inch trays are Tovolo. For more about making cocktail ice, see page 224.

COCKTAIL PICKS
Whether metal, bamboo, or plastic, cocktail picks allow you to enjoy your garnishes without having to fish them out with your fingers.

MEASURING SPOONS
If you want consistent quality and flavor from cocktail to cocktail, we recommend using measuring spoons to measure your bitters (and all amounts less than ¼ ounce). Our favorites are by Cuisipro.

MUDDLER

A muddler is purpose-built for smashing fruit and herbs in a shaker. We prefer an unvarnished wood muddler at least 9½ inches long with a 1½-inch flat head and a comfortable, indented grip. Our winner is the Fletcher's Mill Maple.

JIGGER

A read-from-above graduated jigger with ounce and tablespoon markings (our favorite is Oxo) is best for measuring spirits.

MEASURING CUP

A 1-cup glass liquid measuring cup (our winner is Pyrex) will allow you to measure in ounces, our preferred method.

JUICER

Ban the bottle! Freshly squeezed juice makes superior cocktails. A simple handheld juicer makes quick work of juicing citrus. Our favorite is Chef'n FreshForce.

PARING KNIFE

A small, sharp paring knife is all you need for slicing or chopping fruit and other fresh ingredients for use in cocktails. Our winner is the Victorinox Swiss Army Fibrox Pro.

CHANNEL KNIFE

Use the channel knife part of a zester to make thin citrus twists, which impart a delicate citrus aroma to cocktails. Our favorite is the Messermeister Pro-Touch Combination Zester.

PEELER

A Y-shaped peeler cuts thicker strips of citrus peel for more boldly expressing citrus oils onto the surface of cocktails. Our winner is the Kuhn Rikon Original Swiss Peeler.

RAISE YOUR GLASS

Glassware choice can be utilitarian: A stemmed cocktail glass keeps your hand from warming up a straight-up drink. A short, thick-walled old-fashioned glass allows room for chunky ice cubes and helps insulate your on-the-rocks cocktail. A tall collins glass keeps seltzer bubbles from dissipating too quickly. But beyond the essentials, it's also about tradition, preference, and what vibe you're going for. (For some, it's just not a margarita without a margarita glass!)

ESSENTIAL

COCKTAIL GLASS This iconic glass is needed for shaken or stirred cocktails served straight up (without ice). Choose a 6-ounce V-shaped martini glass or bowl-shaped coupe glass.

OLD-FASHIONED GLASS Also called a rocks glass, this is essential for countless stirred or shaken cocktails served usually (but not always) over ice. We recommend a 12-ounce size.

COLLINS GLASS A tall, narrow 12-ounce collins glass (sometimes called a highball glass) is used for so-called long drinks, which are made with seltzer, juice, or other nonalcoholic mixers.

WINE GLASS A 12-ounce wine glass works just as well as a flute glass in any cocktail situation. We also use it for our Aperol Spritz (page 33) and Peach-Strawberry Frosé (page 156).

PINT GLASS A 16-ounce pint glass is the right size for classic beer-based cocktails like the Michelada (page 34) and for our boozy milkshakes (pages 165 and 166).

MUG An 8-ounce heatproof mug is essential for hot drinks like Irish Coffee (page 43) and Brandied Mulled Cider (page 192).

SPECIALTY

MARGARITA GLASS

A 12-ounce glass is a fun option for all types of frozen drinks (though other glasses such as the old-fashioned or collins can be used instead).

HURRICANE GLASS

For frozen and tiki drinks (especially the Frozen Hurricane, page 159), a 12-ounce version is a good alternative to the Margarita glass.

TIKI GLASS

If you're really into tiki drinks, pick up a funky set of 12-ounce tiki cups or glasses.

FLUTE GLASS

A 6-ounce flute glass is a nice option for Mimosas and Bellinis (page 36), as well as the Fernet Fizz (page 109).

PUNCH CUP

A set of 8-ounce punch cups is great for holiday parties if you have the space for them.

NO. 1
BUILT

Cocktails are built right in the serving glass when they need a gentle mixing treatment, such as drinks with carbonation. Hot drinks can also be built in the glass, since no ice is needed for chilling or dilution.

CONTENTS

FAVORITE GIN
AND TONIC

WHY THIS RECIPE WORKS

The gin and tonic is a classic example of a highball, a family of cocktails made with a spirit and a high proportion of nonalcoholic mixer, typically something sparkling. This essential gin cocktail was born in 19th-century South Asia and Africa, where British colonists drank quinine-rich tonic water to treat malaria. Eventually they added gin, and today this iconic drink is enjoyed around the world. There are multitudes of gins and tonic waters to choose from, from mass-produced to small-batch. We tasted our way through them and agreed on London dry as our favorite gin style, for its crisp, juniper-forward character with a touch of citrus and a whiff of earthiness. To craft a truly superior gin and tonic, worthy of being called our favorite, we developed a Tonic Syrup that was more flavorful than the commercial tonic waters, with all the desirable qualities we wanted—bracing, bittersweet, and boldly perfumed with citrus and grassy notes. And then we stirred together the gin and syrup directly in the glass, topping that mixture with seltzer and just barely stirring to ensure a bubbly G&T. We prefer to use our homemade Tonic Syrup (page 207) and seltzer here; however, you can substitute 6 ounces store-bought tonic water for the syrup and seltzer, if you like.

makes 1 cocktail

- 2 ounces London dry gin
- 1 ounce tonic syrup
- 5 ounces seltzer, chilled
- Lime wedge

Fill chilled collins glass halfway with ice. Add gin and tonic syrup and stir to combine using bar spoon. Add seltzer and, using spoon, gently lift gin mixture from bottom of glass to top to combine. Top with additional ice and garnish with lime wedge. Serve.

LILLET TONIQUE

WHY THIS RECIPE WORKS

Low-alcohol cocktails have always been popular in Europe, especially during the predinner hour as an appetite stimulator. They've become increasingly appreciated in the United States in recent years, and we are big fans of this trend. For this low-alcohol aperitif, we turned to Lillet, an elegant fortified wine from France that has been aromatized with citrus and herbs. It's similar to vermouth in that its alcohol content is greater than that of wine but less than that of a liqueur or a spirit. The original formula, dating to the 1870s, contained quinine (the ingredient that wards off malaria and makes tonic water bitter), but that was removed in the 1980s, making the current iteration of Lillet lighter and more citrus-forward. Traditionally Lillet is served on its own over ice as an aperitif, but we wanted to create a cocktail with it, one that was playful while still maintaining the aromatized wine's air of sophistication. So we decided to put the quinine back in. And our tasters agreed—we initially tried adding fizz via plain seltzer instead of tonic, but they found this version lacking in flavor and complexity. We ultimately discovered that incorporating ¼ ounce of our Tonic Syrup in addition to the seltzer provided a lovely, balanced mix of citrus, herbal, and floral flavors. To garnish, we simply added a lemon slice, which helped emphasize the citrus notes of the Lillet. We prefer to use our home-made Tonic Syrup (page 207) and seltzer here; however, you can substitute 3 ounces of store-bought tonic water for the syrup and seltzer, if you like.

makes 1 cocktail

- 3 ounces Lillet Blanc
- ¼ ounce tonic syrup
- 3 ounces seltzer, chilled
- Lemon slice

Fill chilled wine glass halfway with ice. Add Lillet and tonic syrup and stir to combine using bar spoon. Add seltzer and, using spoon, gently lift Lillet mixture from bottom of glass to top to combine. Top with additional ice and garnish with lemon slice. Serve.

MOSCOW MULE

WHY THIS RECIPE WORKS

The exact origins of the Moscow Mule are up for some debate, but the fact that this cocktail was born out of necessity in the 1940s is not. As the most famous story goes, an overabundance of product triggered a brainstorming meeting between a vodka distributor (John G. Martin) and a friend (Jack Morgan) who owned the Cock 'n' Bull bar in Los Angeles and who also happened to produce his own brand of ginger beer. One night, Cock 'n' Bull bartender Wes Price decided to experiment with these two ingredients that his boss was trying to push. With the addition of lime juice, the Moscow Mule was born. The story continues that Jack Morgan's girlfriend had inherited a copper factory, along with an inventory of poorly selling copper mugs. Thus they decided a copper mug should be the signature vessel for this drink. (A collins glass works just as well, however.) Even if there's some legend in this story, one truth is that this cocktail was responsible for significantly increasing the popularity of vodka in the United States in the mid-20th century. We found the key to a great mule was to add enough potent ginger flavor to temper the strength of the vodka. To achieve that goal, we created a spicy, not-too-sweet Ginger Syrup using both fresh and ground ginger. A splash of lime juice increased the overall brightness of the cocktail by enhancing the gingery snap. We prefer to use 1½ ounces of our homemade Ginger Syrup (page 208) plus 5 ounces of seltzer here, but you can substitute 6 ounces of any premium store-bought ginger beer for the Ginger Syrup and seltzer.

makes 1 cocktail

- 2 ounces vodka
- 1½ ounces ginger syrup
- ½ ounce lime juice, plus lime slice for garnishing
- 5 ounces seltzer, chilled

Fill chilled collins glass or mule mug halfway with ice. Add vodka, ginger syrup, and lime juice and stir to combine using bar spoon. Add seltzer and, using spoon, gently lift vodka mixture from bottom of glass to top to combine. Top with additional ice and garnish with lime slice. Serve.

DARK AND STORMY

WHY THIS RECIPE WORKS

This sweet-spicy cocktail was born in Bermuda just after World War I, the love child of Gosling's Black Seal Rum and some home-brewed ginger beer made by British sailors furloughed on the island. As the story goes, the name originated when a sailor commented that the combination of the black rum (the "dark") and the ginger beer (the "stormy") looked like "the colour of a cloud that only a fool or a dead man would sail under." According-ing to a few trademark certificates on file with the United States Patent and Trademark Office, Gosling's holds the trademark on the name Dark 'n Stormy. For our version, we tested our way through different styles of rum, and it turned out that we preferred the intense color and uniquely deep, burnt sugar–like flavors of Black Seal Rum. (You can substitute your favorite aged rum or another brand of black rum if you like.) Tasters expressed concerns, however, regarding the range of styles and qualities in store-bought ginger beer. Today, store-bought ginger beer is more like soda, a far cry from the traditional bever-age, which is fermented using a wild yeast starter. Popular brands vary greatly in style and flavor, so for our Dark and Stormy, we turned to our own homemade Ginger Syrup. To keep things simple, we built the drink right in the glass (no need to mix up a separate batch of ginger beer), combining the syrup with a splash of fresh lime juice and seltzer water. For the dramatic (you might even say impending) layered presentation, we carefully floated the black rum on top. We prefer to use our home-made Ginger Syrup (page 208) plus seltzer here, but you can substitute 6 ounces of any premium store-bought ginger beer, if desired.

makes 1 cocktail

- 1½ ounces ginger syrup
- ½ ounce lime juice, plus lime wedge for garnishing
- 5 ounces seltzer, chilled
- 2 ounces black rum, such as Gosling's

1 Fill chilled collins glass halfway with ice. Add ginger syrup and lime juice and stir to combine using bar spoon. Add seltzer and, using spoon, gently lift ginger mixture from bottom of glass to top to combine. Top with additional ice, allowing room for rum.

2 Arrange spoon concave side down near surface of ice. Gently pour rum onto back of spoon and into cocktail. Garnish with lime wedge and serve.

AMERICANO

WHY THIS RECIPE WORKS

This gorgeous-looking low-alcohol cocktail is a perfect introduction to the bittersweet charms of Campari and the elegant complexity of sweet vermouth. It's a close relative of the *aperitivo* known as the Milano-Torino, which combines equal parts Campari (from Milan) and vermouth (from Turin). At some point along the way, soda water was added to the "Mi To," as it's known in Italy. Cocktail historians claim this bittersweet, bubbly refresher became known as the Americano when it grew popular among American tourists and expats in Italy during Prohibition. We experimented with various ratios of Campari and vermouth and found that the classic 1-to-1 formula has stood the test of time for an excellent reason. The two main players coexist in perfect balance, the more bitter, astringent qualities of the Campari softened by the gently spiced, sweetly herbal notes of the vermouth. The combination is invigorated by the cooling impact of seltzer and an orange slice. We prefer our homemade Sweet Vermouth (page 244) in this recipe, but you may substitute store-bought sweet vermouth. For a more potent take on the Americano, try the Negroni (page 59), in which gin is substituted for the seltzer—albeit in a smaller quantity!

makes 1 cocktail

1½ ounces Campari
1½ ounces sweet vermouth
 5 ounces seltzer, chilled
    Orange slice

Fill chilled collins glass halfway with ice. Add Campari and sweet vermouth and stir to combine using bar spoon. Add seltzer and, using spoon, gently lift Campari mixture from bottom of glass to top to combine. Top with additional ice and garnish with orange slice. Serve.

APEROL SPRITZ

WHY THIS RECIPE WORKS

Low in alcohol, and with just the right balance between bitter and sweet, the Aperol spritz is one of Italy's most popular *aperitivi*, or predinner cocktails. With its fiery sunset-orange hue, it's also among the most beautiful. This fizzy cocktail was created in the Veneto region of Italy in the 1950s. Sometimes other mildly bitter liqueurs are used instead of Aperol, and we tested a few: Campari made a bolder, more bitter spritz, and Cynar (an artichoke-based *amaro*) made an herbaceous cocktail. But Aperol was our favorite. The secret formula for this liqueur was developed more than 100 years ago; it includes bitter and sweet oranges, herbs, and roots (including rhubarb). The spritz's popularity explosion has generated countless variations made with various ingredients, but we went back to the source for our Aperol Spritz, using the three original components: Aperol, prosecco, and seltzer, gently stirred so as not to lose the fizzy splendor. (Cava or another dry sparkling wine also works well here.) When creating our version, we experimented with different proportions, but tasters agreed that adding 3 parts sparkling wine, along with 2 parts Aperol and 1 part seltzer, achieved the most balanced and complex flavor. Garnishes for the Aperol spritz can be the subject of passionate debate. An orange wedge or peel and green olives are traditional, but these days the olives are often left out, especially outside Italy. In the test kitchen, we appreciated the intriguing salty note a couple of green olives brought to our cocktail, but feel free to omit, if you prefer.

makes 1 cocktail

- 3 ounces dry sparkling wine, such as prosecco or cava, chilled
- 2 ounces Aperol
- 1 ounce seltzer, chilled
  Brine-cured green olives
  Strip of orange peel

Fill chilled wine glass halfway with ice. Add wine, Aperol, and seltzer. Using bar spoon, gently lift mixture from bottom of glass to top to combine. Top with additional ice and garnish with olives, if using. Pinch orange peel over drink and rub outer edge of glass with peel, then garnish with olives and orange peel and serve.

MICHELADA

WHY THIS RECIPE WORKS

Beer is probably not the first thing that comes to mind when you think about cocktails, but there is a well-established tradition of cocktails made with beer. The Michelada is arguably one of the most classic examples of this family of low-alcohol cocktails. It's meant to be drunk on a blisteringly hot day—or as a hangover cure. Originating in Mexico, the Michelada has lots of variations there, depending on what region you're in. The drink made it to America (via Texas) only relatively recently, in the 1990s. American versions often have tomato juice, but in Mexico they are just as likely to omit it. One constant is fresh lime. We found that a generous 2 ounces of lime juice added the refreshing tartness we sought. To balance that tartness, we added doses of Worcestershire sauce and hot sauce, finding that a thicker hot sauce contributed a bit of body. To ensure that everything was well blended, we combined the flavorful seasoning ingredients in the glass before pouring in the beer. Use a well-chilled Mexican lager here. Our favorite is Tecate, but Corona Extra or Modelo will also work. Depending on the size of your glass, you may have some beer left over—we'll let you decide what to do with it. We recommend Cholula and Tapatío hot sauces for their flavor and thicker consistencies. If using a thinner, more vinegary hot sauce such as Tabasco, start with half the amount called for and adjust to your taste after mixing. While we prefer our Sriracha Rim Salt here, you can substitute the Citrus Rim Salt or Herb Rim Salt from page 216 or plain kosher salt.

makes 1 cocktail

- ¼ cup Sriracha Rim Salt (page 217) (optional)
- 2 ounces lime juice (2 limes), plus lime wedge for garnishing
- ½ ounce hot sauce
- ¼ ounce Worcestershire sauce
- 1 (12-ounce) bottle lager, chilled

1 Spread salt, if using, into even layer on small saucer. Moisten about ½ inch of chilled pint glass rim by running lime wedge around outer edge; dry any excess juice with paper towel. Roll moistened rim in salt to coat. Remove any excess salt that falls into glass; set aside.

2 Fill prepared glass halfway with ice. Add lime juice, hot sauce, and Worcestershire and stir to combine using bar spoon. Add beer and, using spoon, gently lift lime mixture from bottom of glass to top to combine. Top with additional ice and garnish with lime wedge. Serve.

MIMOSA

WHY THIS RECIPE WORKS

Champagne-based cocktails date all the way back to the mid-1800s. One of our favorite members of this family is the mimosa, invented in the 1920s at the Ritz in Paris. For our take on this festive, bubbly, brunch-friendly cocktail, we banished even the thought of fruit juice from a bottle or carton, and instead began with equal parts freshly squeezed OJ and, initially, champagne. Tasters loved the fresh citrus—so much so that they wanted more of it, but they also wanted more sparkling-wine flavor. How to do both? A little orange liqueur boosted the orange flavor and added some complexity. We also increased the amount of sparkling wine, which helped ensure a more wine-forward beverage. And we switched to prosecco (or cava) from the far more expensive champagne, with no loss in the quality of the cocktail. We also liked to garnish our Mimosa with an orange slice or twist. The Bellini is a delicious sibling, created in the 1940s in Venice at the legendary Harry's Bar. The original recipe calls for fresh peach puree, but tasters found Bellinis made this way to be too pulpy. Next we tried peach nectar, but it was too sweet. Peach juice proved the ideal route to our favorite Bellini. A little peach schnapps intensified the stone fruit flavor. Our Royal Berry, a riff on the Kir Royale, is more of a cousin than a sibling, in that it involves adding liqueur rather than fruit juice to sparkling wine. We used our mixed-berry Fruits of the Forest Liqueur; however, a store-bought berry liqueur (such as Chambord) will work.

makes 1 cocktail

- 2½ ounces orange juice, plus orange twist for garnishing
- ¼ ounce orange liqueur
- 3 ounces dry sparkling wine, such as prosecco or cava, chilled

Add orange juice and liqueur to chilled wine glass or flute glass and stir to combine using bar spoon. Add wine and, using spoon, gently lift juice mixture from bottom of glass to top to combine. Garnish with orange twist and serve.

ADD A TWIST

Make a **BELLINI** by substituting peach juice for orange juice, and peach schnapps for orange liqueur. Omit orange twist and garnish with fresh peach slice, if desired.

Make a **ROYAL BERRY** by adding 1 blackberry, raspberry, or halved strawberry to bottom of flute glass. Substitute 1½ ounces Fruits of the Forest Liqueur (page 231) for orange juice and orange liqueur. Increase wine to 4 ounces. Omit orange twist.

GRAPEFRUIT-ROSEMARY SPRITZER

WHY THIS RECIPE WORKS

With its citrus and herbal flavors, this simple but sophisticated and not-too-sweet non-alcoholic cocktail is just as much at home on a wintry holiday table as it is at an outdoor summer get-together. The three ingredients add up to far more than just the sum of their parts. We started with 4 ounces of freshly squeezed grapefruit juice and the same amount of seltzer. To temper some of the grapefruit's tartness and enhance the savory backbone of this spirit-free cocktail, we enlisted help from our piney rosemary-infused syrup. Garnish the spritzer with a rosemary sprig in addition to the grapefruit twist, if you like. To create a simple flavor twist on this spritzer, we replaced the grapefruit juice with freshly squeezed orange juice for a sweeter citrus-forward profile and paired the OJ with an earthy thyme syrup for depth of herbal flavor. (And yes, we've also given you a tip on how to turn either version into an alcoholic cocktail.) We prefer to use fresh juice for this spritzer (yellow, pink, or red grapefruit, as you prefer); however, you can substitute unsweetened store-bought juice, if you like.

makes 1 nonalcoholic cocktail

- 4 ounces grapefruit juice, plus strip of grapefruit peel for garnishing
- ½ ounce Herb Syrup with rosemary (page 198)
- 4 ounces seltzer, chilled

Fill chilled collins glass halfway with ice. Add grapefruit juice and herb syrup and stir to combine using bar spoon. Add seltzer and, using spoon, gently lift grapefruit mixture from bottom of glass to top to combine. Top with additional ice. Pinch grapefruit peel over drink and rub outer edge of glass with peel, then garnish with grapefruit peel and serve.

ADD A TWIST

Make an **ORANGE-THYME SPRITZER** by substituting orange juice for grapefruit juice and Herb Syrup with thyme (page 198) for rosemary syrup. Substitute orange peel for grapefruit peel.

Create a traditional cocktail by adding 1 ounce blanco tequila, vodka, or London dry gin to glass with juice.

NEW ENGLANDER

WHY THIS RECIPE WORKS

To create a spirit free beverage that would be equally elegant and festive to serve at either a holiday gathering or a summer beach party, we turned to our Cranberry Shrub Syrup (page 205). Shrubs are acidulated fruit syrups that evolved from the fruit-and-vinegar preserves made by settlers in colonial America. (The term *shrub* actually refers to both the syrup and the drink made from the syrup.) Sweet-tart cranberries are a perfect fruit to receive this sweet-tart shrub treatment. The luscious flavor of the cranberry really shines when mixed with seltzer and a bit of lime juice, resulting in a mocktail that's far more complex and flavorful than the lackluster cranberry-lime combos that make their way into many a glass. (Though we have to admit that we were inspired by the Cape Codder, a venerable old-school cocktail made simply of vodka mixed with cranberry juice and lime, which was invented by Ocean Spray to help market the company's Cranberry Juice Cocktail beverage.) We tested versions of our spirit-free cocktail with additional flavors—ginger, spices, and herbs—but tasters agreed that the bright, fruity flavors of the cranberry syrup were most satisfying when balanced with just the splash of tangy lime juice. The shrub syrup was also sweet enough that we did not need to add any additional sweetener. In a shout-out to our Southern compatriots, we developed a delicious variation using our Peach Shrub Syrup and lemon juice. And yes, you can make either into an alcoholic cocktail by adding—what else?—vodka.

makes 1 nonalcoholic cocktail

- 2 ounces Cranberry Shrub Syrup (page 205)
- ¼ ounce lime juice, plus lime twist for garnishing
- 6 ounces seltzer, chilled

Fill chilled collins glass halfway with ice. Add shrub syrup and lime juice and stir to combine using bar spoon. Add seltzer and, using spoon, gently lift shrub mixture from bottom of glass to top to combine. Top with additional ice and garnish with lime twist. Serve.

ADD A TWIST

Make a **SOUTHERNER** by substituting Peach Shrub Syrup (page 204) for Cranberry Shrub Syrup and lemon juice for lime juice. Omit lime twist and garnish with a fresh peach slice, if desired.

Create a traditional cocktail by adding 1 ounce vodka to glass with shrub syrup.

IRISH COFFEE

WHY THIS RECIPE WORKS

Maybe it's the convivial Irish spirit, or maybe it's because ultimately this is an alcoholic coffee drink decadently topped with whipped cream, but Irish coffee has a tendency to veer toward excess. With many of the versions we sampled, either the ratio of whiskey to coffee was so skewed that you wouldn't be blamed if you forgot there was any coffee to begin with, or they were so sweet you could have ordered them off a dessert menu. Like most great cocktails, the best Irish coffees have balanced flavors, in this case a combination of coffee, Irish whiskey, and sugar. We started by comparing ratios of coffee to whiskey, from 2:1 to 4:1. Surprisingly, tasters agreed that a 4:1 ratio offered the best balance of rich coffee to heady whiskey. Tasters also appreciated a moderate hand when it came to sweetness. Simple syrup was the best choice because of how easily it blended into the coffee mixture. We tested versions made with granulated, brown, and Demerara sugar but found little difference in taste and so stuck with our classic Simple Syrup. The best versions of this drink we tasted featured cream that was whipped enough to float over the drink, but not so stiff that it failed to easily incorporate into the coffee mixture while being enjoyed. Whipping the cream by hand worked best and also provided the best control of thickness. Irish whiskey is traditional here, but rye and Tennessee whiskey also work well. Or take your spiked coffee in a Caribbean or Italian direction by trying one of our twists. We prefer to serve this in a glass mug to highlight the layers of whipped cream and coffee.

makes 1 cocktail

- 2 ounces heavy cream
- ¾ ounce Simple Syrup (page 198), divided
- 4 ounces brewed hot coffee
- 1 ounce Irish whiskey

1 Whisk cream and ¼ ounce simple syrup in chilled bowl until soft peaks just begin to form, about 30 seconds; set aside.

2 Add coffee, whiskey, and remaining ½ ounce syrup to warmed mug and stir to combine. Dollop whipped cream over top. Serve.

ADD A TWIST
Make a **CARIBBEAN COFFEE** by substituting Orgeat Syrup (page 202) for Simple Syrup, and aged rum for whiskey.

Make an **ITALIAN COFFEE** by substituting Citrus Syrup (page 199) with lemon for Simple Syrup, and an amaro, such as Averna, for whiskey.

HOT TODDY

WHY THIS RECIPE WORKS

Toddies have been hailed as a cure-for-what-ails-you for hundreds of years. Arguably the king of hot drinks, the toddy essentially comprises a spirit, hot water, sometimes citrus or spices, and a sweetener (often honey, or maple syrup in Canada, or, in its original form in British-controlled India, fermented palm sap). We don't think a hot toddy should be reserved as only a cold or cough remedy (though many of us in the test kitchen swear by it for that purpose). Made well, it is a delicious cup of comfort to be enjoyed all winter long. And, like many old-school types of drinks, the hot toddy is being seen more and more often, in different iterations, on upscale cocktail menus. Most versions we found varied only slightly between a combination of whiskey or brandy, honey, lemon juice, and hot water. Some versions contained herbal tea, but we preferred to keep our toddy pure and simple. Tasters preferred toddies made with brandy (though bourbon and Tennessee whiskey also worked) and a modest hand when it came to the ratio of brandy to water. As for the lemon juice and honey, we opted for a balanced approach and used an equal amount of each. Don't look for any fancy mixing methods here; just stir everything together, wrap your hands around the steaming cup, and enjoy. Be sure to measure the water after boiling it, since even in the short amount of time it takes to boil, you will lose some to evaporation. In addition to the lemon slice, garnish your toddy with a cinnamon stick, if desired.

makes 1 cocktail

- 5 ounces boiling water
- 1½ ounces brandy
- ½ ounce lemon juice, plus lemon slice for garnishing
- 1 tablespoon honey

Using bar spoon, stir all ingredients together in warmed mug until combined and honey has dissolved. Garnish with lemon slice and serve.

ADD A TWIST
Make a **SCOTCH HOT TODDY** by substituting brewed hot black tea for water and Scotch for brandy.

Experiment with the style of this cocktail by substituting bourbon or Tennesee whiskey for the brandy.

NO. 2

STIRRED

*Stirring with ice before decanting into a serving glass is the best approach
when making spirit-forward cocktails, to gently chill them while avoiding
aeration and protecting against excessive dilution.*

CONTENTS

GIN MARTINI

WHY THIS RECIPE WORKS

The character of a classic gin martini is defined by the delicate balance of botanical flavors and aromas imparted by both gin and dry vermouth. However, the proper balance of these elements is the subject of much discussion. To boot, over decades and across countless bartender reference guides, the ratio of gin to vermouth recommended for a "classic" martini has varied significantly. How "wet" or "dry" a martini is depends on the amount of vermouth; the more vermouth, the wetter the martini. Over time, popular versions of the classic martini have gone from wetter to drier. In older cocktail recipes, martinis approached a nearly equal ratio of gin to vermouth (now referred to as a 50-50 martini). Current fashion calls for ranges from about 2.5:1 to 5:1. Through our testing, we settled on a ratio of 4:1, which allowed tasters to appreciate the distinct flavor notes of both the gin and the vermouth. We favored London dry gin, with its juniper-forward, citrus-tinged flavor profile. To make a drier martini, reduce the vermouth to ¼ ounce; to make a wetter martini, increase it to ¾ ounce. (Or try Julia Child's favorite, the upside-down martini, with 2 ounces of vermouth and 1 ounce of gin.) We prefer our homemade Dry Vermouth (page 242) here, but you can substitute store-bought dry vermouth. We love to garnish our martinis with pimento-stuffed Manzanilla olives. If you prefer, you can substitute (or add) a lemon twist. If you can't find Old Tom gin (which is sweeter and less botanical than London dry gin) to make the Martinez (the drink that begat the martini), you can use London dry gin instead.

makes 1 cocktail

- 2 ounces London dry gin
- ½ ounce dry vermouth
  Brine-cured green olives

Add gin and vermouth to mixing glass, then fill three-quarters full with ice. Stir until mixture is fully combined and well chilled, about 30 seconds. Strain cocktail into chilled cocktail glass. Garnish with olives and serve.

ADD A TWIST

Make a **DIRTY MARTINI** by adding ¼ ounce olive brine to the mixing glass with the gin.

Make a **GIBSON** by decreasing the vermouth to ¼ ounce and substituting cocktail onions for the olives.

Make a **MARTINEZ** by substituting Old Tom gin for the London dry gin, and sweet vermouth for the dry vermouth. Add ¾ ounce maraschino liqueur and ⅛ teaspoon citrus bitters to the mixing glass with the gin. Omit the olives and garnish with a lemon twist.

MANHATTAN

WHY THIS RECIPE WORKS

In terms of status as an icon, stories of cultural lore and legend, and debate over proper formulation, the Manhattan is right up there with the Gin Martini (page 48). In fact, since the Manhattan was actually invented first, you could go so far as to say that the younger martini is essentially a variation on the Manhattan, substituting gin for whiskey and dry vermouth for sweet vermouth, and losing the bitters along the way. Created sometime in the late 1800s, somewhere in Manhattan (possibly at the Manhattan Club, near the current site of the Empire State Building), the major-league, spirit-forward Manhattan is traditionally made from rye, sweet vermouth, and old-fashioned aromatic bitters, garnished with a cocktail cherry. It's infinitely customizable according to the drinker's preference. We loved rye because of how its dry, spicy brashness offset the fruitier sweetness of the vermouth. However, nowadays bourbon is an equally popular choice for the main spirit, and if you choose to go this route you will have a slightly fuller-bodied cocktail with more caramel notes. After deciding on rye, we tested our way through varying amounts of sweet vermouth. The original recipe called for equal parts rye and vermouth, but most modern recipes use more whiskey than vermouth, and tasters agreed this made a more balanced cocktail. The addition of the old-fashioned aromatic bitters helped marry the peppery rye and sweet vermouth for an ultimately strong but smooth cocktail. We prefer our homemade Sweet Vermouth (page 244) in this recipe, but you can use store-bought.

makes 1 cocktail

- 2 ounces rye
- ¾ ounce sweet vermouth
- ⅛ teaspoon old-fashioned aromatic bitters
  Cocktail cherry

Add rye, vermouth, and bitters to mixing glass, then fill three-quarters full with ice. Stir until mixture is fully combined and well chilled, about 30 seconds. Strain cocktail into chilled cocktail glass. Garnish with cherry and serve.

ADD A TWIST

Make a **REVERSE MANHATTAN** by switching the amounts of rye and sweet vermouth.

Make a **MONTE CARLO** by substituting Bénédictine for the sweet vermouth.

Experiment with the style of this cocktail by substituting bourbon, Tennessee whiskey, or Scotch for the rye.

MASTERING STIRRED COCKTAILS

A mixing glass and bar spoon are glamorous conversation pieces in your home bar, and they're fun to use. But they also serve a very practical purpose. Unlike, say, stirring a cup of coffee, applying some technique when stirring cocktails leads to better-tasting drinks.

A mixing glass's straight sides and evenly wide circumference allow for optimal ice movement when stirring. As a result, your drink mixes and chills while being diluted with just enough water to enhance the flavors of the ingredients. Stirred drinks are poured directly into the serving glass, rather than double-strained through a conical strainer as you do with some shaken cocktails (see pages 84–87), and the pouring spout on a mixing glass makes it easier to transfer your cocktail without losing any precious drops. In contrast, the sloped sides and narrower circumference of a Boston shaker are not as conducive to stirring when filled with ice, and the narrower bases of both pieces are not as stable, which can lead to tip-overs. (Trust us on this.)

The elegantly twizzled long-handled bar spoon looks dramatic, but it allows you to stir cocktails efficiently with a few flicks of your wrist. The technique of keeping the outer curved side of the spoon against the wall of the glass while stirring takes a little practice to master, but once you learn it, the spoon will glide around magically, seemingly of its own accord.

HOW TO STIR A COCKTAIL

1 Assemble ingredients in mixing glass, then fill glass three-quarters full with ice.

2 Insert bar spoon into mixing glass with outer curved side positioned against wall of glass. Hold base of mixing glass firmly. Loosely grasp stem of spoon with other hand, between thumb, forefinger, and middle finger (similar to how you would hold a pencil).

3 Pivot wrist of hand holding spoon to guide convex side of spoon around wall of glass, allowing stem of spoon to rotate between your fingers until cocktail is combined and chilled, for the time specified in recipe; remove spoon.

4 Fit julep or Hawthorne strainer into mixing glass and decant drink into chilled serving glass.

OLD-FASHIONED

WHY THIS RECIPE WORKS

The old-fashioned's newfound popularity on cocktail menus owes more than a little something to TV's *Mad Men*. It may have been Don Draper's cocktail of choice in the 1960s, but this American classic has been around since the mid-1800s. At that time, if you walked into a bar and asked for a "whiskey cocktail," you'd get whiskey, sugar, bitters, and ice (or water). Later, as new liqueurs began arriving from Europe and bartenders started experimenting with them, you could no longer be sure what you'd get, so people began asking for a "whiskey cocktail the old-fashioned way." There's debate over whether the old-fashioned was made originally with bourbon or rye—or even rum. (See page 63 for a close cousin of the old-fashioned that uses brandy.) Many recipes call for muddling sugar cubes and fruit in the bottom of a rocks glass, but sugar cube size varies and so using Simple Syrup instead ensured consistency of flavor, and we didn't have to worry about gritty undissolved sugar at the bottom of our cocktail. Old-fashioneds are often sweeter than Manhattans because of that sugar cube, but the small amount of Simple Syrup ensured that ours wouldn't be too sweet. In lieu of the muddled fruit, we discovered that tasters loved the subtle citrus element that citrus bitters brought, in addition to the woodsy notes of old-fashioned aromatic bitters. If you wish, you can use only old-fashioned aromatic bitters in this cocktail, a total of ¼ teaspoon. Either way, since the bitters play a more prominent role here, we prefer our homemade Old-Fashioned Aromatic Bitters (page 210) and Citrus Bitters (page 212), though you can use store-bought.

makes 1 cocktail

- 2 ounces bourbon
- 1 teaspoon Simple Syrup (page 198)
- ⅛ teaspoon old-fashioned aromatic bitters
- ⅛ teaspoon citrus bitters
- Orange twist
- Cocktail cherry

Add bourbon, simple syrup, old-fashioned aromatic bitters, and citrus bitters to mixing glass, then fill three-quarters full with ice. Stir until mixture is just combined and chilled, about 15 seconds. Strain cocktail into chilled old-fashioned glass half-filled with ice or containing 1 large ice cube. Garnish with orange twist and cocktail cherry and serve.

ADD A TWIST
Experiment with the style of this cocktail by substituting rye, Tennessee whiskey, or Scotch for the bourbon.

FANCY FREE

WHY THIS RECIPE WORKS

"Footloose and fancy-free" means having no attachments, romantic or otherwise, but we have to confess that we're pretty attached to this cocktail. The playfully named fancy free is a drink in the style of the old-fashioned, but it's been lightened up a little for those times when you might find the simple but strong nature of the old-fashioned (liquor, sugar, and bitters over ice) not quite up your alley. The recipe for the fancy free first appeared in print in the early 1940s and originally called for serving it straight up, made with bourbon and a sugared rim on the cocktail glass. As with so many cocktails, different versions have made their way into the cocktail lexicon over the years. One constant is that the fancy free uses maraschino liqueur as the sweetening element, rather than the muddled sugar cube or simple syrup of the old-fashioned. The cocktail is a great showcase for this complex cherry liqueur, which is sweetened but has a dry finish. We especially liked it paired with the spicy flavor profile of rye, finding this combination to be a little more complex than that using bourbon. The addition of citrus bitters ensured a pleasantly bright finish. Since the bitters play a larger role in this cocktail, we prefer to use our homemade Citrus Bitters (page 212); however, any store-bought citrus bitters will work.

makes 1 cocktail

- 1½ ounces rye
- ¼ ounce maraschino liqueur
- ¼ teaspoon citrus bitters
-   Strip of orange peel

Add rye, liqueur, and bitters to mixing glass, then fill three-quarters full with ice. Stir until mixture is just combined and chilled, about 15 seconds. Strain cocktail into chilled old-fashioned glass half-filled with ice or containing 1 large ice cube. Pinch orange peel over drink and rub outer edge of glass with peel, then garnish with orange peel and serve.

NEGRONI

WHY THIS RECIPE WORKS

Accepted legend has it that circa 1919, in a bar in Florence, Italy, a particular Count Camillo Negroni ordered his Americano cocktail (page 30) with gin in place of carbonated water. Thus the Negroni cocktail was born, although it took a couple of decades before it appeared in print. Today it's wildly popular, with countless variations and even an entire "Negroni Week" held in cocktail bars worldwide every spring to raise money for charitable causes. Like the Americano, the alcoholic ingredients for the Negroni are mixed in equal parts. (We tested versions made with different ratios of gin, Campari, and sweet vermouth, but we found that given the aromatic intensity of each element, increasing any one in proportion to the others created an imbalance.) The Negroni is considered a classic *aperitivo*, or palate opener, even though the addition of gin makes it stronger than many of the other cocktails in this category. It has a distinct and enjoyable crisp bitterness that pairs perfectly with such savory and piquant appetizers as olives and cheese. We prefer our homemade Sweet Vermouth (page 244) in this recipe, but you can use store-bought sweet vermouth instead, if you like. A single large (2-inch) ice cube looks dramatic in the rocks glass, but alternatively, you can fill the glass halfway with smaller ice cubes of your choice. A single strip of orange peel, its citrus oils carefully expressed into the cocktail just before serving, is the perfect (and classic) garnish.

makes 1 cocktail

- 1 **ounce London dry gin**
- 1 **ounce Campari**
- 1 **ounce sweet vermouth**
   Strip of orange peel

Add gin, Campari, and vermouth to mixing glass, then fill three-quarters full with ice. Stir until mixture is just combined and chilled, about 15 seconds. Strain cocktail into chilled old-fashioned glass half-filled with ice or containing 1 large ice cube. Pinch orange peel over drink and rub outer edge of glass with peel, then garnish with orange peel and serve.

ADD A TWIST

Make a **NEGRONI SBAGLIATO** by substituting chilled, dry sparkling wine, such as prosecco or cava, for the gin. Add Campari and sweet vermouth to chilled wine glass or flute glass and stir to combine using bar spoon. Add wine and, using spoon, gently lift Campari mixture from bottom of glass to top to combine. Garnish with orange peel and serve.

Experiment with the style of this cocktail by substituting bourbon, rye, blanco or reposado tequila, or vodka for the gin.

SAZERAC

WHY THIS RECIPE WORKS

The New Orleans–born Sazerac cocktail gets its name from the cognac—Sazerac de Forge et Fils—used in the earliest versions of the drink. The origin story claims that, in 1838, an apothecary named Antoine Peychaud (a Creole immigrant with a pharmacy in the French Quarter) combined Sazerac cognac with absinthe and a dash of his secret-recipe bitters for his friends. The drink grew in popularity, and in 1850 a bar known as the Sazerac Coffeehouse became the exclusive importer of the Sazerac de Forge et Fils cognac and promoted the cocktail it featured. In 1869, an entrepreneur purchased the bar and founded the Sazerac Company to market spirits, liqueurs, and mixers (including Peychaud's bitters and a bottled version of the Sazerac cocktail) that built upon the iconic cocktail's fame. Eventually, as others tried their hands at crafting the Sazerac, the cognac was replaced by whiskey (usually rye, sometimes bourbon), but the overall formula—lightly sweetened cognac or whiskey with an absinthe wash and a hit of Peychaud's bitters—endured. To perfect our version, we opted for Simple Syrup (over a sugar cube, which is difficult to dissolve). We also developed our Sazerac with absinthe, an intensely aromatic spirit made with anise, fennel, and wormwood, rather than a substitute. Herbsaint (developed by the Sazerac Company when absinthe was banned) or another dry anise-forward liqueur (such as Ricard or dry anisette) can be used. Classic Sazerac recipes call for Peychaud's bitters, but we also recommend swapping in our Cherry-Fennel Bitters (page 213).

makes 1 cocktail

- ½ teaspoon absinthe
- 2 ounces rye
- 1 teaspoon Simple Syrup (page 198)
- ⅛ teaspoon Peychaud's bitters
- Strip of lemon peel

1 Pour absinthe into chilled old-fashioned glass, then tilt and rotate glass to coat interior wall; pour off excess absinthe and set glass aside.

2 Add rye, simple syrup, and bitters to mixing glass, then fill three-quarters full with ice. Stir until mixture is fully combined and well chilled, about 30 seconds. Strain cocktail into prepared glass. Pinch lemon peel over drink and rub outer edge of glass with peel, then garnish with lemon peel and serve.

FIRESIDE

WHY THIS RECIPE WORKS

We especially love to serve—and sip—this cocktail during the autumn months; it just seems appropriate when the leaves are falling and the air has turned chilly. The drink is, essentially, a warmly spiced version of a brandy old-fashioned, a gentler version of the traditional whiskey-based cocktail. Intriguingly, the brandy old-fashioned is the unofficial cocktail of the states of Wisconsin and Minnesota, making those states the two top consumers of brandy in the nation. To make our Fireside, we first replaced the bourbon in our Old Fashioned recipe (page 55) with brandy (for a luxe version, you could even use cognac), which has a flavor profile featuring dried fruit and subtle warm spices. Next, we added a conservative amount of our Spiced Syrup, which is made with cinnamon, cloves, and allspice. These warm baking spices further emphasized the dried fruit flavors in the brandy. Citrus bitters provided the right amount of zingy brightness—think of it as not unlike the lemon juice that's added to the very best spiced apple pie fillings. The optional Pumpkin Pie Spice Rim Sugar will further bump up the warmly spiced elements, plus add a little sweetness. If you like, garnish with a strip of orange peel instead of (or in addition to) the apple slice.

makes 1 cocktail

¼ cup Pumpkin Pie Spice Rim Sugar (page 218) (optional)
  Orange wedge (optional, if using sugar)
2 ounces brandy or cognac
1 teaspoon Spiced Syrup (page 198)
⅛ teaspoon citrus bitters
  Apple slice

1 Spread sugar, if using, into even layer on small saucer. Moisten about ½ inch of chilled old-fashioned glass rim by running orange wedge around outer edge; dry any excess juice with paper towel. Roll moistened rim in sugar to coat. Remove any excess sugar that falls into glass; set aside.

2 Add brandy, spiced syrup, and bitters to mixing glass, then fill three-quarters full with ice. Stir until mixture is fully combined and well chilled, about 30 seconds. Fill prepared glass half-full with ice or add 1 large cube. Strain cocktail into glass. Garnish with apple slice and serve.

OLD POBLANO

WHY THIS RECIPE WORKS

Building from the basic and endlessly customizable template of the old-fashioned (liquor, sugar, and bitters), we wanted to create a cocktail that would have spicy, smoky, sweet complexity. First, we replaced the bourbon in our classic Old-Fashioned recipe with aged rum, which has a nuanced complexity from its time spent in oak barrels, often featuring slightly smoky or vanilla aromas or even raisiny notes. With that style of rum as our base spirit, we suspected that ancho chile liqueur would be a good flavor complement. Ancho chiles, which are dried poblano chiles, bring a subtle, smoky, slow-burn spiciness when infused into a spirit, as compared with a green chile like jalapeño, which has a grassier, cleaner, slap-your-face heat. Our tasters confirmed that ancho was an excellent choice. The ancho liqueur provided a balancing sweetness to the rum while at the same time contributing a welcoming earthy-fruity warmth thanks to the dried chiles. Citrus bitters and a lime peel expressed over the top added a bright element to the finish. We prefer to use our homemade Ancho Chile Liqueur (page 235) here; however, a store-bought dark chile liqueur will work, too.

makes 1 cocktail

- 1½ ounces aged rum
- 1 ounce dark chile liqueur
- ⅛ teaspoon citrus bitters
- Strip of lime peel

Add rum, liqueur, and bitters to mixing glass, then fill three-quarters full with ice. Stir until mixture is just combined and chilled, about 15 seconds. Strain cocktail into chilled old-fashioned glass half-filled with ice or containing 1 large ice cube. Pinch lime peel over drink and rub outer edge of glass with peel, then garnish with lime peel and serve.

NEW-FASHIONED GIN AND TONIC

WHY THIS RECIPE WORKS

The development we did on creating our Tonic Syrup (page 207) caused a spark of creative cocktail inspiration: Was it possible to make a gin and tonic in the style of an old-fashioned, skipping the carbonation (and accompanying dilution) and presenting it instead as a stirred cocktail in a rocks glass? A bit of testing proved that not only was it possible, it was also extremely desirable. This cocktail has all the character of the original gin and tonic, but with a little more backbone and—dare we say—panache. If you think of gin and tonics as strictly summertime drinks, this concentrated version is your entry to serving them year-round. Following the traditional formula, we started with gin but then added tonic syrup only, rather than the customary carbonated tonic water. A few drops of old-fashioned aromatic bitters provided just the right amount of seasoning. We stirred it all together and then poured it over ice. The lime peel garnish was a nod toward a traditional gin and tonic feel and brought in the citrus finish that tasters were looking for. We prefer to use our homemade Tonic Syrup here; however, store-bought tonic syrup will work.

makes 1 cocktail

- 2 ounces London dry gin
- 1½ teaspoons tonic syrup
- ⅛ teaspoon old-fashioned aromatic bitters
  Strip of lime peel

Add gin, tonic syrup, and bitters to mixing glass, then fill three-quarters full with ice. Stir until mixture is just combined and chilled, about 15 seconds. Strain cocktail into chilled old-fashioned glass half-filled with ice or containing 1 large ice cube. Pinch lime peel over drink and rub outer edge of glass with peel, then garnish with lime peel and serve.

ALCACHOFA

WHY THIS RECIPE WORKS

Attention, artichoke lovers, this cocktail is for you! Surprising as it may seem, artichokes are the principal botanical in the beloved Italian *amaro* known as Cynar. Behind the characteristically bittersweet punch that Italian amaro is known for, Cynar's distinctly herbal, vegetal, and woodsy flavor notes are what make it so special. In cocktails, it pairs well with anything from Scotch to orange juice to seltzer, but we loved how it combined with tequila, the deliciously complex Mexican spirit distilled from the blue agave plant, and especially with reposado tequila ("rested" tequila that has been stored for a minimum of two months in the presence of oak). When we tried adding a bit of sweet vermouth to this combination, riffing off of the Negroni (page 59), we found we'd landed squarely on a cocktail known as the alcachofa (from the Spanish word for artichoke). Only in this case, we found that the classic Negroni ratio of 1 (spirit) to 1 (amaro) to 1 (sweet vermouth) left the unique flavor of the Cynar somewhat obscured. After a bit of fiddling, we settled on a more balanced combination that gave our Alcachofa a strong tequila backbone, a clean hit of Cynar, and just enough vermouth to round it out. To add a touch of sweet spice, try gilding the rim of the glass with Smoky Chile Rim Sugar.

makes 1 cocktail

¼ cup Smoky Chile Rim Sugar (page 218) (optional)

Lemon wedge (optional, if using sugar), plus strip of lemon peel for garnishing

2 ounces reposado tequila

¾ ounce Cynar

¼ ounce sweet vermouth

1   Spread sugar, if using, into even layer on small saucer. Moisten about ½ inch of chilled cocktail glass rim by running lemon wedge around outer edge; dry any excess juice with paper towel. Roll moistened rim in sugar to coat. Remove any excess sugar that falls into glass; set aside.

2   Add tequila, Cynar, and vermouth to mixing glass, then fill three-quarters full with ice. Stir until mixture is fully combined and well chilled, about 30 seconds. Strain cocktail into prepared glass. Pinch lemon peel over drink and, if rim is unsugared, rub outer edge of glass with peel. Garnish with lemon peel and serve.

TEATINI

WHY THIS RECIPE WORKS

Can't decide between a cup of tea or a cocktail to cure what ails you? This one's for you. The paths to a tea-based martini-style cocktail were many—with or without vermouth, combining vodka with cold-brewed or chilled hot-brewed tea, adding sweetener or aromatics—but we found that cocktails made using just our homemade Tea Liqueur and vodka featured the refreshingly astringent, bright tea flavor we were after. We attributed this to the extraction power of the vodka we used to make our Tea Liqueur; the tea flavors were much fuller and rounder than those of tea steeped with either hot or cold water. Once we ruled out additional flavoring ingredients, it was just a matter of fine-tuning the ratio of spirits to yield a full-flavored, well-balanced cocktail with just the right amount of sweetness. We liked a ratio of 2 parts vodka to 1 part Tea Liqueur, and since the liqueur already contained Simple Syrup, we did not need to add any other sweetener. A slice of lemon was all it took to finish off this simple yet elegant cocktail. But to add a touch of flair, worthy of taking tea at Kensington Palace, we gilded the rim of the glass with Vanilla Rim Sugar. You can make a Teatini with any black or green tea liqueur.

makes 1 cocktail

¼ cup Vanilla Rim Sugar (page 218) (optional)

Lemon wedge (optional, if using sugar), plus lemon slice for garnishing

2 ounces vodka

1 ounce Tea Liqueur (page 238)

1 Spread sugar, if using, into even layer on small saucer. Moisten about ½ inch of chilled cocktail glass rim by running lemon wedge around outer edge; dry any excess juice with paper towel. Roll moistened rim in sugar to coat. Remove any excess sugar that falls into glass; set aside.

2 Add vodka and liqueur to mixing glass, then fill three-quarters full with ice. Stir until mixture is fully combined and well chilled, about 30 seconds. Strain cocktail into prepared glass. Garnish with lemon slice and serve.

VESPER

WHY THIS RECIPE WORKS

Crisp, botanical and lemony, and strong, the Vesper was initially brought to life on the pages of Ian Fleming's first James Bond novel, *Casino Royale*. Named after 007's ill-fated girlfriend, Vesper Lynd, this cocktail (originally 3 parts gin, 1 part vodka, and 1 part Kina Lillet) gained a resurgence in recent years largely because of the big-screen remake of *Casino Royale* and its follow-up, *Quantum of Solace*. This gin-based drink uses the addition of more neutral-flavored vodka to help lengthen the botanical gin flavor while still allowing the delicate, fruity Lillet to come through. Kina Lillet, which is no longer commercially produced, was an aromatized aperitif wine that contained quinine. Lillet, a similar product that is slightly more citrusy and less bitter, makes an excellent substitute. For our take on this iconic Bond cocktail, we started with the original recipe ratios, but tasters found the drink to be too strong and gin-forward. After testing our way through various combinations, we found that 2 parts gin to 1 part vodka and 1 part Lillet created a more nuanced, well-balanced cocktail. Though originally ordered shaken by Bond (naturally), we stirred our version to avoid too much dilution given the lowered amount of gin. So whether you're a British secret agent saving the world or you're just watching Bond do it on the silver screen, this Vesper is just right for the job.

makes 1 cocktail

- 1½ ounces London dry gin
- ¾ ounce vodka
- ¾ ounce Lillet
- Lemon twist

Add gin, vodka, and Lillet to mixing glass, then fill three-quarters full with ice. Stir until mixture is fully combined and well chilled, about 30 seconds. Strain cocktail into chilled cocktail glass. Garnish with lemon twist and serve.

CHANCELLOR

WHY THIS RECIPE WORKS

We think that a modern revival couldn't happen to a better drink than this magnificent, somewhat forgotten Prohibition-era cocktail. The name alone will make you feel like you're in charge of important things while you're drinking it, but it's also richly delicious. Following the basic template of a "perfect" Manhattan (a variation on the Manhattan made with both sweet and dry vermouth), the Chancellor uses tawny port instead of sweet vermouth, and more significantly, uses Scotch for the whiskey of choice. It's not always easy to get Scotch to play well with others in a cocktail, as its peaty, barley-forward flavor profile can easily dominate, especially when it's the primary liquor. The dried-fruit and caramel flavors of tawny port paired beautifully with the smokier notes of the Scotch, however. Port is a fortified wine from Portugal that uses native grapes; it is aged in wooden casks for at least 3 years (and frequently much longer) before being released for sale, which contributes to its nutty, dried-fruit flavors and brick red–tinged hue. Dry vermouth, with its herbal profile, helped temper some of the port's sweetness, and a final touch of citrus bitters and an orange twist added bright seasoning to this complex, impressively delicious libation.

makes 1 cocktail

- 2 ounces Scotch
- 1 ounce tawny port
- ½ ounce dry vermouth
- 1 teaspoon Simple Syrup (page 198)
- ⅛ teaspoon citrus bitters
- Orange twist

Add Scotch, port, vermouth, simple syrup, and bitters to mixing glass, then fill three-quarters full with ice. Stir until mixture is fully combined and well chilled, about 30 seconds. Strain cocktail into chilled cocktail glass. Garnish with orange twist and serve.

FRENCH KISS

WHY THIS RECIPE WORKS

As we worked with cocktail after cocktail in which vermouth (sweet or dry) complemented and enhanced the protagonists, we found ourselves developing a newfound appreciation for this unsung hero. But it was only when we started developing our own homemade versions of sweet and dry vermouths—learning to appreciate the distinct characteristics of, and interplay among, the many botanical elements—that we decided we were tired of vermouth playing second fiddle. Taking a cue from the vermouth traditions in Italy and Spain, where sweet vermouth is regularly enjoyed as an aperitivo (typically over ice with a bit of orange peel, alongside savory snacks), we explored popular ways of combining sweet vermouth with other elements that gave the vermouth more prominence. Perhaps the most notable of these is the Negroni (page 59), where sweet vermouth is combined in equal parts with gin and Campari, but in that drink the intense flavor of the Campari tends to steal the show. With more research, we found the answer in recipes that called for combining sweet vermouth with an equal measure of dry vermouth. Tasters were delighted; with a lemon twist garnish, our French Kiss cocktail was a keeper. We prefer to use our homemade Sweet Vermouth (page 244) and Dry Vermouth (page 242) in this recipe, but you can substitute your favorite store-bought vermouths.

makes 1 cocktail

1½ ounces sweet vermouth
1½ ounces dry vermouth
    Lemon twist

Add vermouths to mixing glass, then fill three-quarters full with ice. Stir until mixture is just combined and chilled, about 15 seconds. Strain cocktail into chilled old-fashioned glass half-filled with ice or containing 1 large ice cube. Garnish with lemon twist and serve.

NO. 3

SHAKEN

Shaking chills and dilutes cocktails more enthusiastically than stirring, helping to aerate, emulsify, and integrate cocktails that contain juices, cream or milk, or egg whites.

CONTENTS

DAIQUIRI

WHY THIS RECIPE WORKS

Mention a daiquiri, and what comes to mind for many people is a machine-dispensed, sweet and slushy, bright pink, artificially flavored strawberry version they once had on a beach somewhere. Unfortunately, the only part of that description that rings true to the original cocktail is a beach, more specifically one in Cuba: Daiquiri Beach, after which this drink was named. An American engineer working in Cuba at the turn of the 20th century is often credited with first making the daiquiri, although it's more likely that he was just the first to write down a version of a drink that already existed. In any event, not much time passed before it traveled to America. A daiquiri is a classic sour—a family of cocktails built from a spirit, citrus, and sweetener—that is elegant (and delicious) in its simplicity: white rum, lime juice, and sugar shaken until ice-cold, served straight up, and garnished with just a slice of lime. As with other cocktails that traditionally call for granulated sugar, we used our Simple Syrup instead, to ensure a smooth texture in our finished cocktail. We liked the harmonious and classic combination of equal parts lime juice and simple syrup added to a larger amount of white rum, but this formulation is easily adaptable to your preferred levels of sour and sweet.

makes 1 cocktail

- 2 ounces white rum
- ¾ ounce lime juice, plus lime slice for garnishing
- ¾ ounce Simple Syrup (page 198)

Add rum, lime juice, and simple syrup to cocktail shaker, then fill with ice. Shake mixture until fully combined and well chilled, about 15 seconds. Double-strain cocktail into chilled cocktail glass. Garnish with lime slice and serve.

SIDECAR

WHY THIS RECIPE WORKS

The story most often proffered regarding the sidecar's origin is that it was created at Harry's New York Bar in Paris during the First World War for an eccentric American captain who used to arrive at the bar in a chauffeur-driven sidecar. A rival version has it that bar owner Harry MacElhone learned the cocktail at the Buck's Club in London and imported it to Paris, where it fast became a local favorite. Debatable history aside, the sidecar is, at its heart, a member of the daisy family of cocktails: a strong spirit, balanced by citrus and a flavored liquid sweetener, most often in the form of orange liqueur. Does that sound familiar? It should, because the margarita (see page 170) is also a member of the daisy family. In our Sidecar, the warm, aromatic notes of the orange liqueur smooth out the edges of the stronger brandy to make a cohesive and mellow whole. (And if you make our homemade Orange Liqueur on page 228, which we recommend for this cocktail, you actually only need to purchase a single spirit—brandy—to make this drink.) The sugared rim is the traditional garnish for this cocktail. It has fallen out of fashion, but we included it because we loved its celebratory nod to the roaring twenties.

makes 1 cocktail

- ¼ cup sugar (optional)
  Lemon wedge (optional, if using sugar)
- 1½ ounces brandy
- 1 ounce orange liqueur
- ¾ ounce lemon juice, plus lemon twist for garnishing

1 Spread sugar, if using, into even layer on small saucer. Moisten about ½ inch of chilled cocktail glass rim by running lemon wedge around outer edge; dry any excess juice with paper towel. Roll moistened rim in sugar to coat. Remove any excess sugar that falls into glass; set aside.

2 Add brandy, liqueur, and lemon juice to cocktail shaker, then fill with ice. Shake mixture until fully combined and well chilled, about 15 seconds. Double-strain cocktail into prepared glass. Garnish with lemon twist and serve.

MASTERING THE COBBLER SHAKER

This type of shaker came onto the cocktail scene in the later part of the 19th century, several decades after the Boston shaker. An early version of the three-piece cobbler shaker was patented in 1884 by a Brooklynite named of Edward Hauck. He didn't call it a cobbler shaker, but it would soon come to be known by that name, supposedly after the sherry cobbler, one of the most popular cocktails of the day.

Many home bartenders choose the cobbler shaker for its practicality. It's extremely user-friendly—relatively easy to seal and unseal and less likely to leak or otherwise make a mess when you're shaking a drink. Since the strainer is fitted neatly between the cup and the top, when it comes time to serve your cocktail, there's no fiddling with a separate strainer, which can take a bit of coordination and has a higher risk of becoming messy.

But the choice of a cobbler shaker is also a romantic one, a nod to its popularity during the classic era of American cocktails, those decades prior to Prohibition when America went crazy for mixed drinks. It was also the cocktail shaker of choice for 1930s Hollywood, reaching its zenith in the iconic 1934 movie *The Thin Man*.

The three-piece cobbler shaker has always been the default choice in cocktail bars in Japan, where technique is highly prized, and that has contributed to the shaker's resurgence in popularity in America.

HOW TO USE A COBBLER SHAKER

1   Assemble ingredients in base of shaker, then fill with ice.

2   Fit shaker with strainer top and cap to seal.

3   Hold base of shaker firmly with one hand and top of shaker firmly with other hand. Using vigorous back-and-forth motion (ice should hit both ends of shaker), shake cocktail for amount of time specified in recipe.

4   Remove cap (you may need to loosen by gently tapping on counter) and decant cocktail into chilled serving glass, using conical strainer to double-strain if directed.

MASTERING THE BOSTON SHAKER

This type of shaker is older than the cobbler shaker, dating back to the 1840s, though the name Boston shaker doesn't appear in any sources until the 20th century. The metal cup was originally made from tin, but once stainless steel was invented in the first part of the 20th century, it became the metal of choice. And though the mixing glass is certainly breakable, it's generally made from tempered safety glass, so it's superior to your average pint glass.

If you are new to the world of cocktail shakers, the Boston shaker can seem a little intimidating. After all, this is the type of shaker you see professional bartenders in all types of establishments using. But how do you form a tight seal between the metal cup and glass cup so that when you start shaking, you don't end up with your cocktail ingredients all over your kitchen, yourself, or your guests? After shaking, how do you break that seal to release the contents without cracking the glass? And how do you use that separate strainer?

It's true that the Boston shaker takes a little more practice than the cobbler shaker does to master, but if you go this route your time and effort will be rewarded, and you will most certainly earn cocktail cred in the eyes of your guests.

HOW TO USE A BOSTON SHAKER

1   Assemble ingredients in mixing glass, then fill with ice. Invert mixing glass and its contents into shaker tin and angle glass so that one side is flush with tin. Firmly tap base of glass with heel of hand to form tight seal.

2   Hold base of shaker tin firmly with one hand and base of mixing glass firmly with other hand. Using vigorous back-and-forth motion (ice should hit both ends of shaker), shake cocktail as specified in recipe.

3   To break seal, position shaker on counter with mixing glass on top and angled toward you. Grip side of shaker tin with one hand and, using heel of other hand, firmly tap rim of tin on opposite side. (You may have to do this more than once.) Remove mixing glass.

4   Fit Hawthorne strainer onto shaker tin and decant cocktail into chilled serving glass, using conical strainer if directed.

DRY SHAKING

Drinks containing egg whites benefit from an initial "dry" shake (without ice) to break down the egg proteins and develop a light, stable foam. With no ice to cause the metal to chill and contract around the glass, you must modify the technique to ensure a proper seal. Center the mixing glass in the tin rather than angling it flush. Then unseal, add the ice, and seal and shake a second time as directed above. We recommend a Boston shaker for dry shaking, as it has more room to allow for expansion of the egg whites than a cobbler shaker. To preserve the foam, skip the conical strainer when decanting.

HIGHLANDER

WHY THIS RECIPE WORKS

There are classic cocktails, and then there are those cocktails that taste like classics at first sip. The Highlander falls into this latter group for its balance and connection to place. Scotch whiskey is shaken with our Chamomile Liqueur and sweetened with a touch of Herb Syrup made with thyme. The floral, faintly earthy chamomile picks up the grassy herbal quality of the thyme, suggesting heather-laden Scottish Highlands. We veered away from smokier Islay-type whiskeys to preserve the freshness of the drink and preferred the more neutral and balanced counterpoint of a blended Scotch. This drink is based on the principles of the Sidecar (page 83) subfamily of cocktails, which sets a strong spirit against a sweet liqueur and a hefty dose of citrus. Lemon was a natural pairing with the Scotch. We've generally liked serving our shaken drinks straight up in a cocktail glass, as shaking a cocktail will usually dilute the cocktail suffi- ciently. Here, however, we liked how the cocktail evolved and relaxed over ice in a rocks glass, with the drink starting off powerful and concentrated before unwinding in the glass over time. In addition to the lemon peel, you can garnish your cocktail with a fresh thyme sprig, if desired.

makes 1 cocktail

- 1½ ounces Scotch
- ¾ ounce Chamomile Liqueur (page 236)
- ½ ounce lemon juice, plus strip of lemon peel for garnishing
- ¼ ounce Herb Syrup with thyme (page 198)

Add Scotch, liqueur, lemon juice, and herb syrup to cocktail shaker, then fill with ice. Shake mixture until just combined and chilled, about 5 seconds. Strain cocktail into chilled old-fashioned glass half-filled with ice or with 1 large ice cube. Pinch lemon peel over drink and rub outer edge of glass with peel, then garnish with lemon peel and serve.

SOUTHSIDE

WHY THIS RECIPE WORKS

It's too often described in terms of other drinks (such as a gimlet with mint, or as a gin mojito), but we feel the southside deserves to stand proudly on its own. This cocktail may have been invented at a Prohibition-era speakeasy in New York City, or several decades earlier at a swanky hunting and social club (The Southside Sportsmen's Club) on Long Island. Yet another legend has it being created by Prohibition-era gangsters operating on Chicago's South Side to cover up the bad taste of their bootleg gin. But regardless of its origins, the southside is as lovely to drink as it is easy to make. Built in the same fashion as the Daiquiri (page 80)—a classic sour consisting of a spirit, citrus, and sugar—the southside swaps out rum for more-botanical gin. The balance of tart and sweet from lime juice and Simple Syrup is freshened up with a handful of mint added right to the shaker. The mint gets enough bruising during the shaking process to release its aromatic oils into the drink, providing a bright, clean herbaceousness. After one sip of this pale green drink, served elegantly straight up, we think you'll be making this cocktail no matter what geography you find yourself in. While we prefer lime juice in this drink, you can substitute lemon juice with delicious results.

makes 1 cocktail

- 2 ounces London dry gin
- ¾ ounce lime juice
- ¾ ounce Simple Syrup (page 198)
- 8 fresh mint leaves, plus mint sprig for garnishing

Add gin, lime juice, simple syrup, and mint to cocktail shaker, then fill with ice. Shake mixture until fully combined and well chilled, about 15 seconds. Double-strain cocktail into chilled cocktail glass. Garnish with mint sprig and serve.

CORPSE REVIVER NO. 2

WHY THIS RECIPE WORKS

The corpse reviver no. 2 may be the best brunch cocktail you've never heard of. Originally "hair of the dog" drinks designed to cure a hangover, corpse reviver cocktails (there are a few) were developed "to be taken before 11 a.m., or whenever steam and energy are needed," according to *The Savoy Cocktail Book* by Harry Craddock. While cocktails do have a long history of being used for medicinal purposes—the original form of Lillet Blanc, one of this drink's main components, was developed as a more appealing way to consume quinine for malaria treatment—we make no claims as to the restorative (or reviving) properties of this (or any other) cocktail. But we do think its bright, citrusy, herbal, and anise flavors make this a refreshing and unique drink to add to your brunch cocktail rotation. Many recipes use equal parts gin, Lillet Blanc, and orange liqueur; in the kitchen, we preferred a slightly reduced amount of orange liqueur to avoid any pithy, bitter flavor, replacing the lost sweetness with Simple Syrup instead. To amp up the anise notes that pair so well with the citrus and botanical flavors of this drink, we upped the usual dash of absinthe to ⅛ teaspoon. You may use Herbsaint or another dry anise-forward liqueur, like Ricard or dry anisette, in place of the absinthe.

makes 1 cocktail

- 1 ounce London dry gin
- 1 ounce Lillet Blanc
- ¾ ounce orange liqueur
- ¾ ounce lemon juice
- ¼ ounce Simple Syrup (page 198)
- ⅛ teaspoon absinthe
- Orange twist

Add gin, Lillet Blanc, liqueur, lemon juice, simple syrup, and absinthe to cocktail shaker, then fill with ice. Shake mixture until fully combined and well chilled, about 15 seconds. Double-strain cocktail into chilled cocktail glass. Garnish with orange twist and serve.

TARTBREAKER

WHY THIS RECIPE WORKS

For centuries "shrubs," or concoctions of sugared fruit and acid (citrus juice or vinegar) made for drinking, have existed around the world. Possibly originating in Turkey and Persia as a way to preserve fruit, they eventually spread to Europe (particularly England) and then colonial North America, where they often incorporated rum or brandy. With the advent of refrigeration in modern times, using vinegar and sugar to preserve fruit was less essential, and shrubs largely disappeared. But they've recently experienced a renaissance in the cocktail world: Mixed with seltzer (as in our New Englander, page 41), they become refreshing and thirst-quenching nonalcoholic "sodas"; used in cocktails, they become unique before-dinner drinks, as the sour-sweet vinegar flavor stimulates the appetite. For a cocktail made with our Mixed Berry Shrub Syrup, we decided to pair tequila with the floral berry flavors, the shrub syrup bringing sufficient sweetness to enable us to forgo any additional sweetener. Tasters did like just a little lime juice for its fresh zing. Topped with fizzy seltzer, in the style of collins drinks, our bright pink cocktail was as beautiful to look at as it was easy to imbibe, confirming the staying power of shrubs. You can use blanco or reposado tequila in this recipe; reposado will provide more nuanced aged and oaky notes to the drink, while blanco will create a brighter and more tequila-forward cocktail.

makes 1 cocktail

- 2 ounces blanco or reposado tequila
- 1½ ounces Mixed Berry Shrub Syrup (page 204)
- ½ ounce lime juice, plus lime slice for garnishing
- 4 ounces seltzer, chilled

Add tequila, shrub syrup, and lime juice to cocktail shaker, then fill with ice. Shake mixture until just combined and chilled, about 5 seconds. Strain cocktail into chilled collins glass half-filled with ice. Add seltzer and, using bar spoon, gently lift tequila mixture from bottom of glass to top to combine. Top with additional ice. Garnish with lime slice and serve.

ADD A TWIST

Make a **JUST PEACHY** by substituting vodka for the tequila, and Peach Shrub Syrup (page 204) for the Mixed Berry Shrub Syrup. Omit the lime slice and garnish with a fresh peach slice.

MAI TAI

WHY THIS RECIPE WORKS

The most iconic of tiki cocktails, many mai tais served up in bars are a far cry from the original drink developed by Victor Bergeron, or "Trader Vic," in his Polynesian restaurant in Oakland, California, in 1944. It was based on just five ingredients: a singular 17-year-old Jamaican rum, simple syrup, orgeat (a sweet syrup made from almonds and a touch of orange blossom water), orange liqueur, and lime juice. The name "mai tai" derives from the Tahitian phrase for "out of this world—the best." But with the passage of time and changing rum production methods and availability, the mai tai metamorphosed into something less than the best: A variety of inferior rums were substituted, canned pineapple and bottled orange juices frequently made appearances, and umbrellas, neon cherries, and pineapple wedges abounded as garnishes. For our Mai Tai, we preferred a formulation true to the original intent of Trader Vic's drink, using an aged rum and paring down the ingredients to the original list. We also liked the look and aroma of a lime slice and a mint sprig for garnish, but traditionalists may prefer using the spent lime half to create a miniature island with a mint sprig "palm tree" floating in their drink, as Trader Vic envisioned. No matter how you garnish it, we think you'll agree that our Mai Tai lives up to its out-of-this-world origins. We prefer our homemade Orgeat Syrup (page 202) in this recipe; you may substitute a store-bought version, if you like.

makes 1 cocktail

- 2 ounces aged rum
- 1 ounce lime juice, plus lime slice for garnishing
- ¾ ounce orgeat syrup
- ½ ounce Simple Syrup (page 198)
- ½ ounce orange liqueur
- 1 sprig fresh mint

Add rum, lime juice, orgeat syrup, simple syrup, and liqueur to cocktail shaker, then fill with ice. Shake mixture until just combined and chilled, about 5 seconds. Strain cocktail into chilled old-fashioned glass or tiki cup half-filled with crushed ice. Top with additional ice and garnish with lime slice and mint sprig. Serve.

SCORPION CUP

WHY THIS RECIPE WORKS

This fanciful tiki cocktail is traditionally served in a giant bowl for a thirsty straw-wielding crowd. But relegating the scorpion only to large gatherings seemed like a shame to us. We wanted to create a personal-size cocktail that could be enjoyed even when you don't have a big mob in tow. We also wanted to ramp up its quality while still maintaining its party-in-a-flaming-bowl reputation. The versions you get in Chinese-American restaurants frequently feature a mash-up of cheap alcohols, canned fruit juices, and sugary syrups, with various garnishes that sometimes include a "volcano" in the middle consisting of a flaming lime half. After several tastings, we pared down the spirits in our Scorpion Cup to an essential two, with aged rum providing smooth caramel notes and brandy adding a touch of slightly fruity warmth. We preferred fresh orange juice as the primary fruit juice, with fresh lime juice for zingy acidity, grenadine for color and tang, and orgeat for floral nuttiness. Whether garnished simply with cocktail cherries, or with the added bonus of a spectacular flaming lime half, our personal-size scorpion bowl is a drink worthy of being part of your regular cocktail rotation. We prefer our homemade Orgeat Syrup (page 202) in this drink; you can also use a store-bought version, if desired.

makes 1 cocktail

- **2 ounces orange juice**
- **1½ ounces aged rum**
- **½ ounce brandy**
- **¼ ounce grenadine**
- **¼ ounce lime juice**
- **¼ ounce orgeat syrup**
- **Cocktail cherries**

Add orange juice, rum, brandy, grenadine, lime juice, and orgeat syrup to cocktail shaker, then fill with ice. Shake mixture until just combined and chilled, about 5 seconds. Strain cocktail into chilled old-fashioned glass or tiki cup half-filled with crushed ice. Top with additional ice and garnish with cherries. Serve.

ADD A TWIST

Garnish with a flaming rum shot by turning a spent lime half inside out to create a cup. Omit the additional ice and nestle the lime cup in the filled glass. Microwave ½ ounce rum in a small bowl until just beginning to bubble, 10 to 20 seconds. Pour the rum into the lime half and carefully ignite it with a match. Be sure to blow it out before drinking!

SEAPORT SLING

WHY THIS RECIPE WORKS

The sling was one of the earliest categories of cocktails, consisting of a strong spirit, sweetened and diluted in some way. The classic cocktail known as the Singapore sling was the tiki drink before tiki culture existed. The stately colonial-era Raffles Hotel in Singapore lays claim to its origin in 1915, although evidence suggests a longer history. Today, this drink conjures up thoughts of insipidly sweet, supersize cocktails as luridly red as the artificial maraschino cherries that adorn them. That many modern sling recipes contain up to five different sweeteners (such as cherry liqueur, Bénédictine, grenadine, orange liqueur, and pineapple juice) underlies the fact that most are excessively sweet. For our Seaport Sling, we wanted to take this cocktail apart piece by piece. The nonnegotiables were gin and cherry liqueur (such as Heering, different from and not to be confused with maraschino liqueur or kirsch). The honeyed, lightly herbal sweetness of Bénédictine added an intriguing complexity. Grenadine was an easy discard, as its nuance was lost amid the mass of ingredients. Orange liqueur, surprisingly, was not missed either; its citrus oil detracted from the cherry liqueur's singular flavor, lending instead a generic fruit-punch quality. Finally, we investigated some versions without pineapple juice, but we found that we missed its bright, tropical acidity. After trawling through countless recipes, we realized we needed cocktail cherries for our Seaport Sling; we prefer our own (page 223), but store-bought versions may be used. Drambuie may be substituted for the Bénédictine. Garnish with a pineapple slice in addition to the cherries, if desired.

makes 1 cocktail

- 1½ ounces pineapple juice
- 1½ ounces London dry gin
- 1 ounce Bénédictine
- 1 ounce cherry liqueur
- ½ ounce lime juice
- ⅛ teaspoon old-fashioned aromatic bitters
- 2 ounces seltzer, chilled
- Cocktail cherries

Add pineapple juice, gin, Bénédictine, cherry liqueur, lime juice, and bitters to cocktail shaker, then fill with ice. Shake mixture until just combined and chilled, about 5 seconds. Strain cocktail into chilled collins glass or tiki cup half-filled with ice. Add seltzer and, using bar spoon, gently lift pineapple mixture from bottom of glass to top to combine. Top with additional ice and garnish with cherries. Serve.

OMBRÉ SLING

WHY THIS RECIPE WORKS

Flavorful fruit juices, fresh herbs, warm spices, unique syrups, and other mixers are all potential ingredients for nonalcoholic cocktails, making potential flavor combinations seemingly limitless. For this refreshing and fruit-forward creation, we drew inspiration from the Singapore sling, a colorful fruity-herbal gin-based drink that may contain some combination of pineapple, orange, or lime juice, orange liqueur, cherry liqueur, and Bénédictine (an aromatic herbal, honey, and spice liqueur). In our drink, we liked the harmonious ratio of equal parts orange juice and pineapple juice, with just a touch of tart acidity from lime juice to balance their sweetness. To amp up our drink's herbal qualities, we added a handful of fresh mint to the shaker, making our drink distinctively refreshing. Finally, to give our spirit-free cocktail that wow factor, we topped it with a pour of grenadine, which diffused its sweet-tart pomegranate flavor and ruby-red color throughout the entire drink as it gradually settled to the bottom of the glass, creating an ombré effect with shades of light orange, red, and crimson. And since there's no alcohol, we've never been happier to ask for another.

makes 1 nonalcoholic cocktail

- 2½ ounces orange juice
- 2½ ounces pineapple juice
- ½ ounce lime juice
- 12 fresh mint leaves, plus mint sprig for garnishing
- ½ ounce grenadine

Add orange juice, pineapple juice, lime juice, and mint leaves to cocktail shaker, then fill with ice. Shake mixture until just combined and chilled, about 5 seconds. Strain cocktail into chilled collins glass or hurricane glass half-filled with crushed ice. Top with additional ice, then pour grenadine over top, allowing it to settle to bottom of glass. Garnish with mint sprig and serve.

WHISKEY SOUR

WHY THIS RECIPE WORKS

At its simplest, a whiskey sour is whiskey, lemon juice, and sugar, shaken with ice. We think an egg white, a traditional addition that has gone in and out of style over the years, elevates a whiskey sour from good to great. Tasters loved the complexity the egg white brought to this cocktail, adding rich, silky body and foamy frothiness while mellowing the dark spirit. First we gave the ingredients, including the egg white, a "dry shake" (without ice) to emulsify them. Then we added ice to the shaker and gave it a second shake to chill the cocktail. We prefer the spiciness of rye in our Whiskey Sour, but Tennessee whiskey or bourbon also works well. If using one of those alternatives, decrease the Simple Syrup to ¼ ounce. Our twist, the Amaretto Sour, is one of those often-mocked, trendy/not trendy sort of cocktails. But as we learned, a well-made amaretto sour is shockingly delicious. Instead of cocktail cherries in our Amaretto Sour, we loved the extra complexity and sweetness-tempering quality that cherry bitters brought to the drink, especially our homemade Cherry-Fennel Bitters (page 213). For an accurate measurement of egg white, lightly beat a whole egg white in a bowl and then measure out the desired amount. While we enjoy the creamy mouthfeel that the egg white adds to these cocktails, it can be omitted (or replaced; see our egg-free twist). We prefer to use a Boston shaker for this recipe, as it typically has more room than a cobbler shaker for the expansion of the egg white foam in step 1. For more information on dry-shaking a cocktail, see page 86.

makes 1 cocktail

2 ounces rye
1 ounce egg white
½ ounce Simple Syrup (page 198)
½ ounce lemon juice
Cocktail cherries

1 Add rye, egg white, simple syrup, and lemon juice to cocktail shaker and vigorously shake until mixture is foamy, 30 to 45 seconds.

2 Fill shaker with ice, then shake mixture until fully combined and well chilled, about 15 seconds. Strain cocktail into chilled cocktail glass. Garnish with cherries and serve.

ADD A TWIST

Make an **AMARETTO SOUR** by substituting amaretto for the rye. Omit the Simple Syrup and increase the lemon juice to 1 ounce. Add ⅛ teaspoon cherry bitters to the shaker with the amaretto.

If you are concerned about the egg white, you may substitute aquafaba (the liquid drained from canned chickpeas). Skip step 1 and shake all the ingredients together with ice as directed in step 2.

RAMOS GIN FIZZ

WHY THIS RECIPE WORKS

Our Ramos Gin Fizz will wow you with its good looks as much as it will with its flavor—which is showstoppingly delicious. A New Orleans original, this cocktail has a gin, simple syrup, and lemon juice base but adds egg white and heavy cream, which, when shaken and topped with seltzer, create a luscious levitating layer of foam that is like a meringue crossed with an ice cream soda. There's a romantic notion that making this cocktail is a thing of legend, requiring fleets of bartenders to pass the cocktail shaker from one to the next for the 10 minutes of shaking purportedly required. In our tests, we found that extended shaking of this cocktail actually resulted in foam with a curdled, overwhipped texture. Instead, we turned to dry-shaking everything except the ice, cream, and seltzer to maximize the aeration before wet-shaking with the added ice and cream to chill and emulsify the drink. Pouring the cocktail over some of the chilled seltzer gently created the signature top layer of foam, and allowing the cocktail to rest before slowly topping it with the remaining seltzer created a sturdier, denser foam that rose above the edge of the glass (we found that a longer rest led to a more dramatic presentation). The orange blossom water contributes an ethereal aroma and flavor; look for it in the international aisle of well-stocked supermarkets or in Indian or Middle Eastern markets. For an accurate measurement of egg white, lightly beat a whole egg white in a bowl and then measure out the desired amount. We prefer to use a Boston shaker for this recipe, as it typically has more room than a cobbler shaker for the expansion of the egg white foam in step 1. For more information on dry-shaking a cocktail, see page 86.

makes 1 cocktail

- 2 ounces London dry gin
- 1 ounce Simple Syrup (page 198)
- 1 ounce egg white
- ½ ounce lemon juice
- ½ ounce lime juice
- ⅛ teaspoon orange blossom water
- 1½ ounces heavy cream
- 5 ounces seltzer, chilled, divided

1 Add gin, syrup, egg white, lemon juice, lime juice, and orange blossom water to cocktail shaker and vigorously shake until foamy, 30 to 45 seconds.

2 Add cream to shaker, then fill with ice. Shake mixture until fully combined and well chilled, about 30 seconds.

3 Pour 3 ounces seltzer into chilled collins glass. Strain cocktail into glass and let rest for at least 30 seconds or up to 2 minutes. Slowly pour remaining 2 ounces seltzer into glass (foam will rise above rim). Serve.

ADD A TWIST
If you are concerned about the egg white, you may substitute aquafaba (the liquid drained from canned chickpeas). Skip step 1 and shake all ingredients together with cream and ice as directed in step 2.

FERNET FIZZ

WHY THIS RECIPE WORKS

Sharply medicinal and aggressively aromatic, fernet is a divisive beverage. It's the most notorious member of the amaro family, a group of digestivi that consist of spirits (or in some cases wine) that have been infused with multiple herbs, roots, barks, and spices and sweetened to varying degrees. They can range in style from the low-proof, sweet-bitter Aperol to the full-on Fernet-Branca, which is 78 proof, barely sweetened, and oak-aged. Fernet has become the cultish favorite of the barkeeping world, where industry insiders celebrate the end of a difficult shift with a round. We wanted to put this amaro into a cocktail that would please even the most ardent naysayers. Looking around the world for inspiration, we discovered that fernet and cola is the de facto national drink of Argentina. Intrigued at the prospect of what syrupy soda could do to tame the amaro, we set to work. It was a nonstarter, as tasters found that the acidic cola exacerbated the most astringent elements of the fernet. We did like the bubbles, so we switched to seltzer. Bourbon was an excellent spirit pairing, as its sweet charred-oak elements melded with the fernet. Tasters agreed that the egg white was essential, giving a softer mouthfeel and a beautiful pearlescent head. For an accurate measurement of egg white, lightly beat a whole egg white in a bowl and then measure out the desired amount. We prefer to use a Boston shaker for this recipe, as it typically has more room than a cobbler shaker for the expansion of the egg white foam in step 1. For more information on dry-shaking a cocktail, see page 86. We prefer Fernet-Branca here, but you may use another fernet, if you like.

makes 1 cocktail

- 1 ounce bourbon or Tennessee whiskey
- ½ ounce egg white
- ½ ounce Fernet-Branca
- ½ ounce Simple Syrup (page 198)
- ¼ ounce lemon juice, plus lemon twist for garnishing
- ⅛ teaspoon citrus bitters
- 1½ ounces seltzer, chilled

1 Add bourbon, egg white, Fernet-Branca, simple syrup, lemon juice, and bitters to cocktail shaker and vigorously shake until mixture is foamy, 30 to 45 seconds.

2 Fill shaker with ice, then shake mixture until fully combined and well chilled, about 15 seconds. Strain cocktail into chilled wine glass or flute glass. Slowly pour seltzer over top of cocktail. Garnish with lemon twist and serve.

ADD A TWIST
If you are concerned about the egg white, you may substitute aquafaba (the liquid drained from canned chickpeas). Skip step 1 and shake all ingredients together with ice as directed in step 2.

LIMONTINI

WHY THIS RECIPE WORKS

Limoncello is a bracing, sweet-yet-refreshing Italian liqueur typically enjoyed chilled on its own as a *digestivo*, at the end of a meal to stimulate digestion. To enjoy it in a simple vodka martini–style cocktail is another pleasure altogether—drier and more subdued, our elegant Limontini is designed to be imbibed before your meal, along with a few bites of something savory, to awaken the appetite. We tested numerous combinations of limoncello, vodka, vermouth, simple syrup, and bitters, but time and time again tasters chose the simple combination of vodka and limoncello. Adding a bit of lemon juice to punch up this duo encouraged the sweet-tart citrus liqueur to shine without distraction. So to perfect our drink, it was simply a matter of finding the right ratio: 1 ounce of limoncello to 1½ ounces of vodka provided just the right amount of sweetness and lemony bite. To accentuate the citrus aroma even more, we garnished our Limontini with a simple twist. We strongly prefer to use our homemade Limoncello in this simple recipe, but you may substitute your favorite store-bought limoncello.

makes 1 cocktail

- 1½ ounces vodka
- 1 ounce Limoncello (page 232)
- ¼ ounce lemon juice, plus lemon twist for garnishing

Add vodka, limoncello, and lemon juice to cocktail shaker, then fill with ice. Shake mixture until fully combined and well chilled, about 15 seconds. Double-strain cocktail into chilled cocktail glass. Garnish with lemon twist and serve.

ADD A TWIST
Make an **ARANTINI** by substituting Arancello (page 232) for the Limoncello. Garnish with lemon or orange twist.

AVIATION

WHY THIS RECIPE WORKS

The aviation brings to mind a golden age of new frontiers, when exotic air travel was the purview of the (very) leisured classes. This is indeed a cocktail from that golden age, as we can trace its origin to at least as far back as 1916. Sleek and sophisticated, and with a touch of the unknown, it's a gin sour that has been softened by maraschino liqueur, with crème de violette adding a floral undertone. The cocktail in its original form vanished mid-century, as crème de violette was no longer available in the United States. Its fortunes shifted during the cocktail renaissance, when drinkers clamored for pre-Prohibition drinks, and the forgotten liqueur was once again imported from Europe. We tried a version without the violette, but tasters were unimpressed. The key to balance in this cocktail is the interplay between its alcoholic strength and its delicate floral quality. All the recipes we saw called for a very small amount of the violette, as many warned of the risks of adding too much and having the drink veer into hand-soap territory. However, the violette was hard for tasters to discern. We found that we could balance additional liqueur with slightly less sweetener and more lemon juice to preserve its distinct character without it becoming overwhelming. You can substitute ¼ ounce Lavender Liqueur (page 236) for the crème de violette if desired, but increase the Simple Syrup to ½ ounce. A lemon twist makes a nice additional garnish, if desired.

makes 1 cocktail

- 2   ounces London dry gin
- ¾   ounce lemon juice
- ½   ounce crème de violette
- ¼   ounce maraschino liqueur
- ¼   ounce Simple Syrup (page 198)
-     Cocktail cherries

Add gin, lemon juice, crème de violette, liqueur, and simple syrup to cocktail shaker, then fill with ice. Shake mixture until fully combined and well chilled, about 15 seconds. Double-strain cocktail into chilled cocktail glass. Garnish with cherries and serve.

BICHON FRISE

WHY THIS RECIPE WORKS

One would never guess that the delicate, lacy, starry white flowers of the elderberry bush would create such an explosion on the cocktail scene. Though they have been used medicinally and culinarily in Europe for centuries, it wasn't until 2007 that elderflower liqueur—primarily in the form of the liqueur named St-Gemain—showed up widely in cocktails in the United States. And did it ever. Perfumed with aromas reminiscent of lychee, pear, and citrus, elderflower liqueur adds a touch of floral sophistication to a drink, and it became the secret (or not-so-secret) weapon in many a bartender's arsenal. For our elderflower cocktail, we paired it with neutral vodka to let the elderflower flavors shine through, and with complementary grapefruit juice to add pleasing bitterness. But grapefruit juice can be too much of a blunt instrument on its own; a touch of lemon juice brightened up the drink and ultimately enhanced and intensified the grapefruit flavor. Why name this elegant drink after a dog (albeit a cute, white, fluffy one)? The combination of vodka and grapefruit juice is a greyhound; add elderflower and a squeeze of lemon and it becomes our Bichon Frise; add a vanilla sugar–rimmed glass and it becomes exquisite. We prefer our Vanilla Rim Sugar for this drink, but plain granulated sugar will also work. We prefer freshly squeezed red grapefruit juice; unsweetened bottled grapefruit juice can also be used.

makes 1 cocktail

¼ cup Vanilla Rim Sugar (page 218) (optional)

   Grapefruit wedge (optional, if using sugar)

1½ ounces vodka

1 ounce red grapefruit juice, plus strip of grapefruit peel for garnishing

¾ ounce elderflower liqueur

¼ ounce lemon juice

1   Spread sugar, if using, into even layer on small saucer. Moisten about ½ inch of chilled cocktail glass rim by running grapefruit wedge around outer edge; dry any excess juice with paper towel. Roll moistened rim in sugar to coat. Remove any excess sugar that falls into glass; set aside.

2   Add vodka, grapefruit juice, liqueur, and lemon juice to cocktail shaker, then fill with ice. Shake mixture until fully combined and well chilled, about 15 seconds. Double-strain cocktail into prepared glass. Pinch grapefruit peel over drink and, if rim is unsugared, rub outer edge of glass with peel. Garnish with grapefruit peel and serve.

TUMBLEWEED

WHY THIS RECIPE WORKS

Infused into a liqueur, ancho chiles (which are dried ripe poblano peppers) can add an unexpected additional dimension to a cocktail—a mild, smoky, earthy heat that lingers at the end of each sip. And where better to add a touch of heat than a sweet-spicy-sour riff on a classic margarita? Margaritas are traditionally made with tequila, orange liqueur, and lime juice, and, in our opinion, they are hard to improve upon (see our Best Fresh Margaritas on page 170). But swapping out the traditional orange liqueur for ancho liqueur, and adding guava nectar along with the lime juice, gave us a brand-new, unique combination that was pleasantly tart at the start and smoky with just a bit of heat at the finish. Guava nectar is an attractive pink beverage with a thicker consistency than juice and a tangy flavor that has hints of pear, grapefruit, and strawberry. To reinforce the dark chile flavors from the liqueur, we added a rim of chile-infused sugar. You can find guava nectar in the international aisle (or the juice aisle) of most well-stocked supermarkets. We prefer to use our homemade Ancho Chile Liqueur (page 235) here, but any store-bought dark chile liqueur will work. We prefer our Smoky Chile Rim Sugar for the sugared rim, but you may substitute plain granulated sugar. You can use blanco or reposado tequila in this recipe; blanco will create a brighter and more tequila-forward cocktail, while reposado will provide more nuanced aged and oaky notes to the drink.

makes 1 cocktail

- ¼ cup Smoky Chile Rim Sugar (page 218) (optional)
- Lime wedge (optional, if using sugar)
- 1½ ounces guava nectar
- 1 ounce blanco or reposado tequila
- ½ ounce dark chile liqueur
- ¼ ounce lime juice, plus lime slice for garnishing
- 1 ounce Simple Syrup (page 198)

1 Spread sugar, if using, into even layer on small saucer. Moisten about ½ inch of chilled cocktail glass rim by running lime wedge around outer edge; dry any excess juice with paper towel. Roll moistened rim in sugar to coat. Remove any excess sugar that falls into glass; set aside.

2 Add guava nectar, tequila, liqueur, lime juice, and syrup to cocktail shaker, then fill with ice. Shake mixture until fully combined and well chilled, about 15 seconds. Double-strain cocktail into prepared glass. Garnish with lime slice and serve.

COCOCHAI

WHY THIS RECIPE WORKS

There are many reasons to shake a cocktail: to chill, to dilute, to mix all the ingredients properly, and to add texture. Yet it is the drink's texture change that is the most thrilling result. For example, a heavy, oily cocktail can become light but mouth-filling as shaking helps incorporate air into the drink's body. And with a little help from an egg white, a foam as creamy as that of any cappuccino can be created to add further textural contrast. This is true for nonalcoholic cocktails as well, and we wanted to create one as textural and foamy as any cocktail that needed neither eggs nor alcohol to make it great. We were inspired by Vietnamese coffee, a traditional drink in which lower-density coffee naturally floats above higher-density condensed milk. In our "upside-down" version, the milk is layered instead on top of spiced black tea. In testing, we found that the amount of condensed milk needed to create a distinct layer made the drink unpalatably sweet. So we tried a different tack and switched to canned coconut milk, which, when shaken, created gorgeous open bubbles with a frothy texture that was rich but light. Wanting more complexity, we brewed our own chai, an Indian drink made by simmering black tea with any number of spices, but cardamom, cinnamon, and cloves are the most prevalent. All together, this blend made for a pantry-friendly, highly gluggable spirit-free cocktail for any time of day or night. This recipe makes enough chai for four drinks.

makes 1 nonalcoholic cocktail

- 18 ounces water
- 3 black tea bags
- 1 (1-inch) piece ginger, sliced thin
- ½ cinnamon stick, plus extra for garnishing
- 5 green cardamom pods, lightly crushed
- 5 peppercorns
- 3 whole cloves
- 1 ounce Simple Syrup (page 198)
- 4 ounces coconut milk
- ¼ teaspoon vanilla extract

1 Bring water to simmer in small saucepan over medium-high heat. Stir in tea bags, ginger, cinnamon stick, cardamom pods, peppercorns, and cloves and simmer for 5 minutes. Strain chai through fine-mesh strainer into small bowl, gently pressing on tea bags to extract as much liquid as possible; discard solids. Let chai cool to room temperature, then transfer to airtight container and refrigerate until chilled, at least 1 hour or up to 1 week.

2 Fill chilled collins glass halfway with ice. Add 3 ounces of chai and simple syrup and stir to combine using bar spoon. Top with additional ice, leaving room for coconut milk.

3 Add coconut milk and vanilla to cocktail shaker, then fill with ice. Shake mixture until frothy, about 15 seconds. Arrange spoon concave side down near surface of ice. Gently pour coconut mixture onto back of spoon and into cocktail. Grate extra cinnamon stick over top and serve.

ESPRESSO MARTINI

WHY THIS RECIPE WORKS

Drinks based on combinations of coffee and spirits abound throughout the world, but perhaps none is quite as elegant as the espresso martini. Traditionally consisting of vodka, espresso, and coffee liqueur, this style of "martini" is shaken (not stirred) to create a thin layer of foam—or crema—just as one would find on a hot espresso. Served in a martini glass with a garnish of three floating espresso beans, this drink was the height of sophistication when it was developed in the 1980s in London. For our updated take on this modern classic, we swapped out the vodka for smooth aged rum, and added Bénédictine (a French liqueur based on 27 different herbs, spices, and plants), which added notes of warm spice, honey, and vanilla. After combining these two ingredients with the bitter, chocolaty flavors of brewed espresso and coffee liqueur, we felt our cocktail was equally appealing as an after-dinner sip or as a cocktail hour pick-me-up before a special evening out; we'll let you decide. This cocktail tastes best with freshly made and chilled espresso, but you can substitute ½ teaspoon of instant espresso powder dissolved in 1 ounce hot water, if necessary. We strongly prefer to use our homemade Coffee Liqueur here, but any store-bought coffee liqueur will work.

makes 1 cocktail

- 1½ ounces aged rum
- 1 ounce brewed espresso, chilled, plus espresso beans for garnishing
- ¾ ounce Bénédictine
- ½ ounce Coffee Liqueur (page 241)

Add rum, espresso, Bénédictine, and liqueur to cocktail shaker, then fill with ice. Shake mixture until fully combined and well chilled, about 15 seconds. Double-strain cocktail into chilled cocktail glass. Garnish with espresso beans and serve.

ADD A TWIST
Make a **LATTETINI** by adding ½ ounce heavy cream to the shaker with the rum.

MUDDLED

Crushing raw elements such as fruit, vegetables, and herbs in the shaker or mixing glass encourages them to release their flavors, aromas, and colors into cocktails.

CONTENTS

MOJITO

WHY THIS RECIPE WORKS

Origin stories for the mojito range from it being invented during Sir Francis Drake's attempted plunder of Cuba in 1586 to it being concocted in a Havana bar that Ernest Hemingway frequented in the 1950s. But while the origins of the mojito are unclear, the deliciousness of this king of muddled drinks is not. Fresh and herbaceous from muddled mint, sweet yet tart from fresh lime juice and sugar, and with a kick of white rum and a fizzy splash of seltzer, the mojito is perennially popular, and it's easy to see why. Yet there are some versions of a mojito that we'd rather not drink again: those with a crunchy layer of undissolved sugar at the bottom, and those where we have to strain out shreds of muddled mint with our teeth. To solve the first problem, we muddled a generous amount of mint with Simple Syrup instead of granulated sugar to ensure that the sweetener was fully dissolved in the cocktail. Muddling the mint for a full 30 seconds, until it was fragrant, extracted maximum mint flavor even without the help of abrasive granulated sugar. To avoid shreds of herb clogging up our straw or our teeth, we did all the muddling in a cocktail shaker, added the remaining ingredients and ice to shake, and then strained it all into a chilled serving glass over ice. Topped with chilled seltzer and garnished with a fresh sprig of mint, our drink was both refreshing and easy to drink.

makes 1 cocktail

- ⅓ cup fresh mint leaves, plus mint sprig for garnishing
- 1 ounce Simple Syrup (page 198)
- 2 ounces white rum
- ¾ ounce lime juice
- 4 ounces seltzer, chilled

1 Add mint leaves and simple syrup to base of cocktail shaker and muddle until fragrant, about 30 seconds. Add rum and lime juice, then fill shaker with ice. Shake mixture until just combined and chilled, about 5 seconds.

2 Double-strain cocktail into chilled collins glass half-filled with ice. Add seltzer and, using bar spoon, gently lift rum mixture from bottom of glass to top to combine. Top with additional ice and garnish with mint sprig. Serve.

CAIPIRINHA

WHY THIS RECIPE WORKS

The caipirinha is widely, though somewhat inaccurately, known as the daiquiri of Brazil. While it's true that the cocktail is made simply from sugarcane rum, limes, and sugar, the nuance of the ingredients and the methodology set it apart. The main ingredient, cachaça, is often thought of as a type of rum, since both are made from sugarcane. However, whereas true rum is made from molasses (a by-product of sugarcane), cachaça is made by distilling fermented sugarcane juice, which makes it more similar to *rhum agricole* (French Caribbean rum). Cachaça is less refined than most rums, lending it a grassier flavor. Historically it was considered a rough spirit, and so one story of the caipirinha's origin is that the liquor needed enough lime and sweetness to mask its coarseness. Cachaça production techniques have improved so much that it is now considered a fine spirit, and many premium aged bottles exist on the market. These higher-quality bottles are slowly making their way to the United States. Whereas Americans are used to the caipirinha being served over crushed ice, in Brazil it is always stirred with cubed ice. In either case, the first step is muddling lime pieces, often with granulated sugar. We found a technique to muddle limes, then shake them with ice and Simple Syrup in order to fully incorporate the citrus and sweetener. Then, for the best of both worlds, we dumped it all straight into a glass without straining: This gave us a few pleasantly crunchy nuggets of cracked ice with some whole ice cubes that didn't overdilute the drink. Any cachaça will work with this drink, but we prefer the depth of flavor from an aged cachaça.

makes 1 cocktail

- 1 lime, halved crosswise, each half quartered
- 2 ounces cachaça
- ¾ ounce Simple Syrup (page 198)

Add lime pieces to base of cocktail shaker and muddle until broken down and all juice has been expressed, about 30 seconds. Add cachaça and simple syrup, then fill shaker with ice. Shake mixture until just combined and chilled, about 5 seconds. Pour contents of shaker into chilled old-fashioned glass (do not strain). Serve.

MASTERING MUDDLED COCKTAILS

Originally known as toddy sticks, muddlers are one of the oldest purpose-built cocktail tools, dating back more than 200 years. They were originally used to crush chunks of sugar into water for toddies and other early cocktails like juleps. Their purpose has evolved over the years, but the basic design of today's muddlers hasn't changed much, although they can be made from stainless steel or plastic as well as from wood.

Muddling quickly infuses fresh flavor elements from solid ingredients directly into a cocktail: Think of the cooling sensation of crushed mint, the lingering heat of smashed ginger, or the intensity of citrus peel. This simple technique creates exciting opportunities for flavor pairings because of the range of ingredients that you can muddle. Fresh herbs, spices, fruits, and even vegetables are all fair game.

Muddling technique is not complicated. We found that about 30 seconds was sufficient time to crush any of our raw ingredients, releasing their juices or expressing their aromatic oils. (Longer muddling times can occasionally lead to "swampy" flavors, especially if muddling fresh herbs.) So whether it's a mojito, a mint julep, or a muddled creation of your own, break out your muddler and let the creative juices flow.

HOW TO MUDDLE FRESH HERBS

1   Add herb leaves and Simple Syrup, if using, to base of cocktail shaker or mixing glass.

2   Hold cocktail shaker or mixing glass firmly with one hand. Gripping muddler with other hand, press firmly into herbs, rotating handle slightly as you progress, until herbs are broken down and fragrant, about 30 seconds.

HOW TO MUDDLE FRESH FRUITS AND VEGETABLES

1   Cut fruit or vegetables into small pieces, then add to base of cocktail shaker or mixing glass.

2   Hold cocktail shaker or mixing glass firmly with one hand. Gripping muddler with other hand, press firmly into fruit, rotating handle slightly as you progress, until fruit is broken down and all juice has been expressed, about 30 seconds.

CELERY GIMLET

WHY THIS RECIPE WORKS

Celery flavoring a cocktail? Stay with us here. Muddled in a cocktail, celery adds refreshing and subtle grassy notes and a beautiful pale green color, creating a sophisticated and unique drink. We chose a classic gimlet—a bright and tart cocktail traditionally made with gin and lime cordial (sweetened lime juice)—in which to muddle celery, knowing that the vegetal flavors of the celery would complement the gin's botanical notes. We tested both celery stalks and leaves to see which would provide the most pronounced flavor, finding that muddled stalks gave the best fresh but delicate celery flavor, which paired beautifully with the zingy lime and the herbal notes of the gin. While gimlets—originally used in the British navy as an appetizing way to prevent scurvy by giving sailors vitamin C–rich lime juice—are now frequently made with sweetened bottled lime cordial, we preferred the flavor of fresh lime juice and Simple Syrup. If you'd like to explore muddled gimlets further, try arugula (yes, really!). Muddled arugula makes a vibrant green drink with a pleasantly peppery aroma and bite; we replaced the traditional gin with vodka to encourage the arugula flavors to shine through.

makes 1 cocktail

- 1 small celery rib, chopped, plus celery leaf for garnishing
- ¾ ounce Simple Syrup (page 198)
- 2 ounces London dry gin
- ¾ ounce lime juice

Add celery and simple syrup to base of cocktail shaker and muddle until celery is broken down and all juice has been expressed, about 30 seconds. Add gin and lime juice, then fill shaker with ice. Shake mixture until fully combined and well chilled, about 30 seconds. Double-strain cocktail into chilled cocktail glass. Garnish with celery leaf and serve.

ADD A TWIST
Make an **ARUGULA GIMLET** by substituting ⅓ cup of baby arugula for the celery, and vodka for the gin. Garnish with an additional arugula leaf.

AUTUMN IN NEW ENGLAND

WHY THIS RECIPE WORKS

There are times when cocktails showcase interesting and unexpected combinations—one wonders at the temerity of the bartender who first dropped a pickled onion into a glass of hard liquor (page 48)—and then there are ingredients that, when combined, taste like they were always meant to be together. Apple and sage are one such pairing: The piney, slightly astringent notes of the sage are mellowed and made whole by the bright sweetness of apples. Whereas a decent ⅓ cup of leaves was generally required for cocktails using milder herbs such as mint or basil, that much sage entirely overwhelmed this cocktail. We gently muddled just a couple of sage leaves in maple syrup to infuse our sweetener with herbal flavor. Then we shook this up with some apple cider (whose sweet, slightly fermented flavor added even more depth) and smoky, caramel-y bourbon. As is, this was too sweet, and so we sought something acidic to balance things out. First we turned to lemon, as it has a relatively neutral flavor that allows other components to shine. But then we struck upon using a little cider vinegar instead, in keeping with the apple theme. Its clean, bracing acidity worked perfectly, adding another touch of savoriness to this round, juicy cocktail. Garnish with sage and, if you like, a slice of apple. If your sage leaves are longer than 2 inches, use the lesser amount.

makes 1 cocktail

- 2-4 fresh sage leaves, plus small sage sprig for garnishing
- ¼ ounce maple syrup
- 2 ounces bourbon
- 1 ounce apple cider
- ¼ ounce cider vinegar

Add sage leaves and syrup to base of cocktail shaker and muddle until fragrant, about 30 seconds. Add bourbon, apple cider, and vinegar, then fill shaker with ice. Shake mixture until just combined and chilled, about 5 seconds. Double-strain cocktail into chilled old-fashioned glass half-filled with ice or containing single large ice cube. Garnish with sage sprig and serve.

HOLE IN ONE

WHY THIS RECIPE WORKS
Iced tea with lemon is one of the most refreshing summer drinks we know, and we aren't the only ones who think so: A mix of equal parts lemonade and iced tea is known as an Arnold Palmer, named after the legendary pro golfer who favored this combination after a long day on the course. Ordering a John Daly will get you the same combination, plus vodka. Unfortunately, often that cocktail is heavily sweetened or made with flavored mixes rather than with real ingredients. We had a hunch that a muddled version of this drink made with fresh lemons and our homemade Tea Liqueur would be far better—as excellent as, well, a hole in one. To get the most lemon flavor, we muddled a cut lemon to extract all of its bright acidity and citrusy aroma. Initially we then added only the Tea Liqueur—our version made from black tea infused into vodka—along with Citrus Syrup made with lemon, and shook our drink until it was well combined and frosty. After some tasting, we found that we needed to balance the tea and lemon flavors further, because too much Tea Liqueur made the drink tannic and astringent. So we incorporated some plain vodka. Pouring the entire contents of the shaker right into the glass, with seltzer to top everything off, resulted in a citrusy, tart, and refreshing tea and lemon cocktail perfect for summer sipping. We prefer our homemade Tea Liqueur made with black tea in this recipe, but store-bought versions will also work.

makes 1 cocktail

¼ lemon, cut into 4 pieces, plus lemon slice for garnishing

1½ ounces Tea Liqueur (page 238)

1 ounce vodka

¾ ounce Citrus Syrup with lemon (page 199)

2 ounces seltzer, chilled

1   Add lemon pieces to base of cocktail shaker and muddle until broken down and all juice has been expressed, about 30 seconds. Add liqueur, vodka, and citrus syrup, then fill shaker with ice. Shake mixture until just combined and chilled, about 5 seconds.

2   Pour contents of shaker into chilled collins glass (do not strain). Add seltzer and, using bar spoon, gently lift tea mixture from bottom of glass to top to combine. Top with additional ice and garnish with lemon slice. Serve.

TONGUE THAI'D

WHY THIS RECIPE WORKS

What are the elements that make for a good nonalcoholic cocktail? It's definitely easier to lay out what is not successful: It shouldn't just be a hodgepodge of different fruit juices that work well together—that concoction would merely be a juice blend. There needs to be something to differentiate and elevate it further, whether achieved through balancing the fruit with bitter, sweet, or spicy flavor elements or incorporating texture with syrups or muddled ingredients. Here we selected four fragrant Thai basil leaves and muddled them with lime-based Citrus Syrup for a fresh aromatic base with just a hint of anise (any more basil and the flavor overwhelmed the balance of the drink). Muddling half a seeded Thai chile with the basil swathed the cocktail in spice. We used coconut water for the bulk of the drink's liquid, imparting a sweet, nutty-yet-fresh flavor. Then it was just a matter of evening out the cocktail's acidity with a good slug of lime juice, which lent a tropical brightness. This amalgamation gave us something balanced, with a definite chile kick and flavors that were firmly rooted in Thai cuisine. We were all very happy to slowly sip this distinctly grown-up, spirit-free cocktail. Italian basil can be substituted for the Thai basil. For a less spicy cocktail, you can shake the chile along with the coconut water and lime juice, rather than muddling it with the basil.

makes 1 nonalcoholic cocktail

- 4 fresh Thai basil leaves
- 1 Thai chile, halved and seeded, divided
- ¼ ounce Citrus Syrup with lime (page 199)
- 3 ounces coconut water
- ½ ounce lime juice

Add basil leaves, half of chile, and citrus syrup to base of cocktail shaker and muddle until fragrant, about 30 seconds. Add coconut water and lime juice, then fill shaker with ice. Shake mixture until fully combined and well chilled, about 30 seconds. Double-strain cocktail into chilled cocktail glass. Garnish with remaining chile half. Serve.

KIWI BLOSSOM

WHY THIS RECIPE WORKS

At first glance, kiwi and cucumber may seem like unlikely bedfellows, vivid green coloring aside. However, the sweet-tart kiwifruit (which actually hails from China rather than New Zealand) evokes a kind of tropical melon with crunchy, strawberry-like seeds. The cucumber, with its intense freshness, similarly echoes flavors of melon—to which it's related, both being members of the cucurbit family. So their pairing actually makes a lot of sense. Muddling proved a great way to unlock their flavors. Initially we liked the idea of not straining the drink so that the flesh of the fruit could add a little body. But the kiwi seeds were everywhere (there can be as many as 1,500 in a single fruit!), so we strained them out (it's fine if a few seeds make it through the strainer). We thought this the perfect cocktail for showcasing our homemade Jasmine Liqueur: Its heady, deeply fragrant aroma perked up the delicate, balanced combination of cucumber and kiwi. And like kiwi, the jasmine plant originally comes from China. We found we needed to cut the intense liqueur with a little vodka to keep its strong floral qualities from overwhelming the mild fruits. We finished with a splash of seltzer to further lighten this kiwi-hued cocktail that seems so perfect for hot summer days. Garnish with a cucumber slice in addition to the kiwi slice, if desired.

makes 1 cocktail

½ kiwi, quartered, plus kiwi slice for garnishing

1 (1-inch) piece English cucumber, quartered

1½ ounces Jasmine Liqueur (page 236)

1 ounce vodka

½ ounce Simple Syrup (page 198)

¼ ounce lemon juice

3 ounces seltzer, chilled

1 Add kiwi and cucumber to base of cocktail shaker and muddle until broken down and all juice has been expressed, about 30 seconds. Add liqueur, vodka, simple syrup, and lemon juice, then fill shaker with ice. Shake mixture until just combined and chilled, about 5 seconds.

2 Strain cocktail into chilled collins glass half-filled with ice. Add seltzer and, using bar spoon, gently lift jasmine mixture from bottom of glass to top to combine. Top with additional ice and garnish with kiwi slice. Serve.

SICILIAN SOJOURN

WHY THIS RECIPE WORKS

In the depths of winter, when the already limited variety of available fruit all seems so pale and tasteless, citrus is one of the bright spots in the produce section. And blood oranges are a particularly beautiful and flavorful winter standout. Their crimson to deep garnet flesh gets its color from anthocyanins, the same powerful antioxidant found in blueberries. Blood oranges, which are a bit smaller than regular oranges, originated in the southern Mediterranean and feature prominently in southern Italian (specifically Sicilian) and Spanish cuisine. When juiced, these oranges make for a striking dark magenta drink with flavor notes of raspberries and just a touch of grapefruit-style bitterness. For our refreshing and flavorful nonalcoholic cocktail with blood oranges, we turned to fresh tarragon, the anise-licorice notes of the herb forming a classic combination with citrus that is found in many a Mediterranean dish. Muddling a couple tablespoons of the herb in Simple Syrup gave us plenty of tarragon flavor, and adding freshly squeezed blood orange juice and a touch of lemon juice balanced the sweetness and acidity. Poured over ice and topped with chilled seltzer, our beverage was rich in citrus flavor, with a unique herbal back note and a beautiful color to brighten even the darkest winter day. You can substitute fresh basil for tarragon, if you like. If you can't find blood oranges, you can substitute navel oranges.

makes 1 nonalcoholic cocktail

- 2 **tablespoons fresh tarragon leaves, plus tarragon sprig for garnishing**
- 1 **ounce Simple Syrup (page 198)**
- 3½ **ounces blood orange juice (3 oranges)**
- ¼ **ounce lemon juice**
- 4 **ounces seltzer, chilled**

1   Add tarragon leaves and simple syrup to base of cocktail shaker and muddle until fragrant, about 30 seconds. Add orange juice and lemon juice, then fill shaker with ice. Shake mixture until just combined and chilled, about 5 seconds.

2   Double-strain cocktail into chilled collins glass half-filled with ice. Add seltzer and, using bar spoon, gently lift juice mixture from bottom of glass to top to combine. Top with additional ice and garnish with tarragon sprig. Serve.

BUBBLES AND BLOOMS

WHY THIS RECIPE WORKS

Muddling is a quick and effective way to impart the fresh flavors, aromas, and colors of fruits to a cocktail. Berries in particular can add striking color, as they do here, where muddled blueberries make for an eye-catching fuchsia-hued drink. We chose vodka for our base spirit so that its neutral flavor would enhance rather than compete with the floral and fruity additions. To build upon our elegantly pink cocktail, we incorporated elderflower liqueur, a sophisticated, delicate concoction made from the white flowers of the elderberry bush; it has honeyed, citrusy flavor notes of lychee and pear. Adding a small amount of Simple Syrup and a touch of lemon juice ensured balanced brightness. To send this cocktail over the top, after shaking and straining it into a cocktail glass, we topped our drink with a pour of fizzy sparkling wine, adding festive effervescence. Raspberries or blackberries may be substituted for the blueberries. We developed this recipe using fresh blueberries for muddling, but garnishing it with frozen berries of your choice is a lovely way to keep the cocktail chilled.

makes 1 cocktail

- 2 tablespoons blueberries
- ½ teaspoon Simple Syrup (page 198)
- 1 ounce vodka
- 1 ounce elderflower liqueur
- ¼ ounce lemon juice
- 2 ounces dry sparkling wine, such as prosecco or cava
  Frozen blueberries, raspberries, or blackberries

Add blueberries and simple syrup to base of cocktail shaker and muddle until berries are broken down and all juice has been expressed, about 30 seconds. Add vodka, liqueur, and lemon juice, then fill shaker with ice. Shake mixture until fully combined and well chilled, about 30 seconds. Double-strain cocktail into chilled cocktail glass. Top with sparkling wine and garnish with frozen berries. Serve.

MINT JULEP

WHY THIS RECIPE WORKS

Served in a frosted silver julep cup and topped with a mound of crushed ice and a fragrant, bountiful bouquet of mint, the mint julep became the official drink of the Kentucky Derby in 1938. But while mint juleps are inexorably tied to Kentucky, they may have had their origins more than a century earlier in Virginia, where mint was mixed with brandy or rum as a medicinal morning pick-me-up. Regardless of its lineage, this three-ingredient cocktail (four counting the ice) is elegant in its simplicity and is meant to be sipped, the flavors and intensity of the drink evolving as the crushed ice melts. For our take on this iconic cocktail, we didn't stray far from the classic composition: We muddled a third of a cup of fresh mint leaves with Simple Syrup to release the aromatic oils, and stirred in bourbon and ice before straining the cocktail into a serving vessel (an old-fashioned glass works if you don't have a julep cup) and topping with a mound of crushed ice and a generous sprig of fresh mint. Tasters enjoyed the fresh minty flavor and the slight, but not too strong, sweetness. For a different take, we swapped out mint for basil and bourbon for rye, creating a spicier flavor profile. If you'd like even a little more kick, try our gingery smash version, where we muddled coins of fresh ginger and used Tennessee whiskey to create a spicy-sweet icy drink.

makes 1 cocktail

- ⅓ **cup fresh mint leaves, plus mint sprig for garnishing**
- ½ **ounce Simple Syrup (page 198)**
- 2 **ounces bourbon**

1 Add mint leaves and simple syrup to mixing glass and muddle until fragrant, about 30 seconds. Add bourbon, then fill glass three-quarters full with ice. Stir until mixture is just combined, about 15 seconds.

2 Double-strain cocktail into chilled old-fashioned glass or julep cup half-filled with crushed ice. Top with additional crushed ice to form mound above rim of glass. Garnish with mint sprig and serve.

ADD A TWIST

Make a **RYE-BASIL JULEP** by substituting basil for the mint, and rye for the bourbon. Garnish with a basil sprig.

Make a **WHISKEY-GINGER SMASH** by substituting 1 (1-inch) piece of fresh ginger, sliced thin, for the mint, and Tennessee whiskey for the bourbon. Garnish with an additional ginger slice.

BLENDED

Cocktails requiring a blender are usually, but not always, frozen drinks. The blender is used to puree some or all of the ingredients, which adds body and texture to the cocktail, whether frozen or not.

CONTENTS

BOURBON-CHERRY SLUSH

WHY THIS RECIPE WORKS

Cherry slush from the ice cream truck ranks among the fondest of summertime childhood memories for many of us in the test kitchen. We wanted to have a little fun and create a thoroughly grown-up version of this icy treat to help recall thoughts of those simpler times. Starting with a full pound of frozen sweet cherries guaranteed strong, delicious cherry flavor while ensuring this cocktail wouldn't be seasonally dependent. The next step was deciding on the best liquor to use. Because the red-fruit flavor of cherries goes so well with the oaky, caramel-vanilla notes of bourbon (think about the old-fashioned or the Manhattan), this whiskey seemed like it would be the clearly favored choice for our adult slush, and that proved true in testing. (Tennessee whiskey was a close runner-up.) To add a touch of tartness to balance the rich flavors of the cherries and bourbon, we turned to frozen orange juice concentrate. The OJ boosted that fruity, fun flavor we've come to expect from traditional (that is, nonalcoholic) slush. For a more complex flavor profile, we added several drops of old-fashioned aromatic bitters. With every frosty sip, this Bourbon-Cherry Slush conjured up that familiar ice cream truck jingle and reminded us that, even as grown-ups, it's good to relax and enjoy lazy summers in the present.

makes 4 cocktails

- 8 ounces bourbon
- ½ cup frozen orange juice concentrate
- 1 teaspoon old-fashioned aromatic bitters
- 1 pound (4 cups) frozen sweet cherries
- 20 ounces (5 cups) ice cubes
  Orange wedges
  Cocktail cherries

Add bourbon, orange juice concentrate, bitters, cherries, and ice to blender (in that order) and process until smooth, about 1 minute, scraping down sides of blender jar as needed. Pour into chilled old-fashioned glasses. Garnish with orange wedges and cocktail cherries and serve.

PIÑA COLADAS

WHY THIS RECIPE WORKS

The official drink of Puerto Rico, this magical combination of pineapple, coconut, and rum can be enjoyed either shaken over ice or frozen. We wanted to create a frozen version bursting with real tropical fruit flavor. With that in mind, we first compared fresh pineapple, frozen pineapple, canned pineapple, and pineapple juice. Tasters found the natural flavor of fresh pineapple more appealing than the processed flavor of canned or juice. Since we were making a frozen drink, frozen pineapple (fresh fruit frozen at its peak of ripeness) offered the best of both worlds, providing the flavor of fresh while reducing the amount of additional ice needed for texture. Next we experimented with cream of coconut, coconut milk, and coconut cream. Many recipes call for cream of coconut, but tasters thought this made the drink taste like sunblock. Coconut milk was too thin and watery. We ultimately chose coconut cream for its great mouthfeel and rich, natural coconut flavor. As for the rum, choosing from the array of colors and grades was no easy task (though it was a fun one). White rum provided just the right flavor, holding its own with the pineapple and coconut without overpowering them. For a dramatic presentation that adds complexity, we suggest floating some aged rum on top. Do not substitute cream of coconut for the coconut cream, as the former is heavily sweetened.

makes 4 cocktails

- 1 (15-ounce) can coconut cream
- 6 ounces white rum
- 2 ounces Simple Syrup (page 198)
- 12 ounces (3 cups) frozen pineapple chunks
- 8 ounces (2 cups) ice cubes
  Fresh pineapple slices

Add coconut cream, rum, simple syrup, pineapple, and ice to blender (in that order) and process until smooth, about 1 minute, scraping down sides of blender jar as needed. Pour into chilled old-fashioned glasses or hurricane glasses. Garnish with pineapple and serve.

ADD A TWIST

Add a rum float by arranging bar spoon concave side down near surface of cocktail. Gently pour ½ ounce aged rum onto back of spoon and into cocktail.

FROZEN MARGARITAS

WHY THIS RECIPE WORKS

The world's first frozen margarita machine made its debut in Dallas in 1971, vaulting Tex-Mex restaurants into the popular consciousness and making this festive frozen drink America's most popular cocktail, surpassing the martini. Now it's a mainstay companion for nachos, tacos, and more. If you only know the sickly sweet, too-icy machine slush, get ready for a revelation. Our frozen version has tangy, true citrus flavor and a perfect consistency. Rather than squeezing, sweetening, and freezing juice from fresh limes, we opted for the convenience of frozen limeade concentrate (made with real limes), which offered the ideal sweet-tart balance and also helped create the ideal semifrozen texture when combined with ice. We then tested our way to the best, most balanced proportions of citrus to alcohol. While we prefer using our Citrus Rim Salt here, you can substitute another flavored rim salt from page 216 or plain kosher salt. You can use blanco or reposado tequila in this recipe; reposado will provide more nuanced aged and oaky notes to the drink, while blanco will create a brighter and more tequila-forward cocktail.

makes 4 cocktails

- 2 tablespoons Citrus Rim Salt (page 216) (optional)
  Lime wedges
- 6 ounces blanco or reposado tequila
- 4 ounces orange liqueur
- 1 (12-ounce) container frozen limeade concentrate
- 20 ounces (5 cups) ice cubes

1 Spread salt, if using, into even layer on small saucer. Moisten about ½ inch of 4 chilled old-fashioned glass or margarita glass rims by running lime wedge around outer edges; dry any excess juice with paper towel. Roll moistened rims in salt to coat. Remove any excess salt that falls into glasses; set aside.

2 Add tequila, orange liqueur, limeade concentrate, and ice to blender (in that order) and process until smooth, about 1 minute, scraping down sides of blender jar as needed. Pour into prepared glasses. Garnish with lime wedges and serve.

FLORENTINE FREEZE

WHY THIS RECIPE WORKS

In any Italian piazza in the predinner hour, at any time of year, you will find friends catching up over *aperitivi*. Often that early evening drink is a Negroni (page 59). But for scorching summer days, we wanted to create a frozen riff on this classic cocktail, which is traditionally equal parts Campari, gin, and sweet vermouth. To lighten up the strong flavors a bit, we opted to use fruit juice in place of the vermouth. In testing several varieties of juice, tasters unanimously preferred citrus, and specifically orange juice, since the sweet flavor of the orange juice tempered both the herbal spiciness of Campari and the botanical notes of the gin. But simply dumping a lot of ice into the blender along with the juice and other ingredients resulted in a disappointingly soupy, decidedly unslushy concoction. A trick we learned during our testing of frozen drinks was to swap out fresh juice in favor of frozen concentrate. So we tried that here, and the orange juice concentrate added its sweet flavor to the Campari and gin while at the same time helping to create the proper smoothly icy texture without excess dilution of flavor. Proving that not all frozen drinks need to be sweet-tart, our Florentine Freeze achieved a complex herbal-bittersweet flavor that tasters deemed *molto delizioso*.

makes 4 cocktails

4   ounces Campari
4   ounces gin
1   (12-ounce) container frozen
    orange juice concentrate
20 ounces (5 cups) ice cubes
    Orange slices

Add Campari, gin, orange juice concentrate, and ice to blender (in that order) and process until smooth, about 1 minute, scraping down sides of blender jar as needed. Pour into chilled collins glasses. Garnish with orange slices and serve.

PEACH-STRAWBERRY FROSÉ

WHY THIS RECIPE WORKS

Frosé, frozen rosé wine blended with other ingredients, is a hip new kid on the cocktail block, having become popular only in the past couple of years. But oh how popular it is! People can't seem to get enough of this pretty, pink, fruit-forward wine cocktail, and with good reason. Though you may see it churning away in countertop machines at restaurants, it's simple to make at home. While some recipes call for pouring wine right from bottle to blender, we discovered that freezing some of the wine first in ice cube trays created the best slushy texture. Many recipes call for strawberries and lemon juice, but we found this to be overwhelming. Instead, combining equal parts strawberries and peaches resulted in a light, fresh fruitiness that enhanced rather than suppressed the flavor of the wine. We used frozen fruit (fruit picked at the peak of ripeness and then frozen); this, along with the wine ice cubes, eliminated the need for adding regular ice cubes (which, in testing, caused the frosé to have an unpleasantly icy consistency). The risk of brain freeze has never been more worth it! Use a fruitier rather than a drier rosé for this cocktail.

makes 4 cocktails

1   **(750-ml) bottle rosé wine**
3   **ounces Simple Syrup (page 198)**
4½ **ounces (1 cup) frozen strawberries**
4½ **ounces (1 cup) frozen peaches**
    Fresh strawberry slices

1   Measure out and reserve 10 ounces wine. Divide remaining wine between 2 ice cube trays and freeze until firm, about 2 hours. (Frozen wine cubes can be transferred to zipper-lock bag and kept frozen for up to 2 months.)

2   Add reserved wine, simple syrup, strawberries, peaches, and frozen wine cubes to blender (in that order) and process until smooth, about 1 minute, scraping down sides of blender jar as needed. Pour into chilled wine glasses. Garnish with strawberry slices and serve.

ADD A TWIST

Make **PEACH FRIESLING** by substituting sweet (*spätlese*) Riesling for rosé, omitting strawberries, and increasing peaches to 2 cups.

Add complexity to this cocktail by substituting citrus or herb syrups (see pages 198–199) for Simple Syrup.

FROZEN HURRICANES

WHY THIS RECIPE WORKS

The hurricane is one of the most famous tiki drinks created in America in the 1940s during the simultaneous rum glut and whiskey shortage of World War II. (Rum from the Caribbean was easier to obtain than whiskeys from Europe.) The creation of this relative of the daiquiri is credited to New Orleans tavern owner Pat O'Brien, and it's one of many iconic cocktails famously associated with the Big Easy. However, the frozen versions you typically find floating down Bourbon Street these days are pumped from giant machines, mix-based, garishly red from dye, and laden with artificial ingredients and harsh, cheap booze. For our Frozen Hurricanes, we wanted to bring this drink back to its quality roots. We poured through many iterations with various fruit juices in them and eventually narrowed our version down to three: passion fruit, orange, and lime. To get the frozen consistency just right, ice alone wasn't enough, so we adjusted our cocktail with frozen passion fruit puree and a freezer staple, orange juice concentrate. This drink typically has a combination of rums, but after testing several mixtures, we discovered that we preferred just one type in our Frozen Hurricanes: aged rum, which provided deep, rich flavor while still allowing the fruit juices to shine. A bit of sweetness from grenadine balanced the sour notes of the passion fruit, keeping this frozen rum punch delightfully balanced.

makes 4 cocktails

- ½ cup frozen passion fruit puree
- ½ cup frozen orange juice concentrate
- 8 ounces aged rum
- 1½ ounces lime juice (2 limes), plus lime wedges for garnishing
- 1½ ounces grenadine
- 16 ounces (4 cups) ice cubes
- Cocktail cherries

Add passion fruit puree, orange juice concentrate, rum, lime juice, grenadine, and ice to blender (in that order) and process until smooth, about 1 minute, scraping down sides of blender jar as needed. Pour into chilled old-fashioned glasses or hurricane glasses. Garnish with lime wedges and cocktail cherries and serve.

HORCHATA BORRACHA

WHY THIS RECIPE WORKS

Every household and restaurant in Mexico boasts its own version of wildly popular horchata. This traditional milky drink is typically made by steeping raw rice, and sometimes various nuts or seeds, in water with warm spices, then blending the mixture to creamy goodness. It's the perfect complement to spicy Mexican cuisine or fantastic on its own—no wonder tasters were easily hooked in the test kitchen. Our *borracha* ("drunken") version started traditionally enough, but we found that adding almonds to the rice base lent more complex flavor and a creamier feel to the beverage. We combined water, almonds, sugar, and rice with vanilla extract and cinnamon. Letting the mixture soak overnight not only softened the nuts and rice (making blending easier) but also deepened the flavor infusion. Then we blended the mixture until the rice and almonds broke down. The addition of heavy cream helped make the horchata even creamier (tests of half-and-half revealed insufficient creaminess, while sweetened condensed milk made the drink too sweet). Our spirit of choice for our Horchata Borracha was clear: The lighter body and tropical toasted-sugar flavors of white rum were ideal.

makes 4 cocktails

- 20 ounces water
- 5 ounces whole, slivered, or sliced blanched almonds
- ½ cup sugar
- ¼ cup long-grain white rice
- ¾ teaspoon vanilla extract
- ½ teaspoon ground cinnamon, plus extra for garnishing
- ¼ teaspoon table salt
- 6 ounces white rum
- 4 ounces heavy cream
- Lime slices

1   Combine water, almonds, sugar, rice, vanilla, cinnamon, and salt in bowl. Cover and let sit at room temperature for at least 12 hours or up to 24 hours.

2   Set fine-mesh strainer over 8-cup liquid measuring cup and line with triple layer of cheesecloth that overhangs edges. Process almond mixture in blender until smooth, 30 to 60 seconds, scraping down sides of blender jar as needed.

3   Transfer mixture to prepared strainer and let drain until liquid no longer runs freely, about 5 minutes. Pull edges of cheesecloth together to form pouch, then firmly squeeze pouch to extract as much liquid from pulp as possible; discard pulp. You should have 2 cups liquid. Stir in rum and cream, cover, and refrigerate until completely chilled, at least 1 hour or up to 2 days. Stir to recombine, then pour into chilled collins glasses filled with ice. Garnish with lime slices and cinnamon and serve.

FROZEN WATERMELON COOLERS

WHY THIS RECIPE WORKS

On a hot summer's day, watermelon in any form is a quintessential thirst quencher. So, transforming this succulent fruit into a vibrant, crowd-pleasing nonalcoholic cocktail seemed like a no-brainer. We initially started by simply combining fresh watermelon chunks and ice in a blender. Tasters found the semislushy consistency pleasing, but the ice diluted most of the delicate watermelon flavor. Next we tried freezing half the watermelon pieces before blending; this nicely replicated the preferred semislushy consistency without compromising the watermelon flavor. We accented our fruit base with fresh lime juice for a lightly sweet and tangy profile. Just a little bit of Simple Syrup, balanced by some salt, enhanced the watermelon and brought out the sweet and tart flavors even further. After blending everything for just a minute, we had the perfect sippable poolside beverage. Depending on the sweetness of your watermelon, you may need to add the greater amount of Simple Syrup. While we prefer using our Citrus Rim Salt here, you can substitute another flavored rim salt from pages 116–117, or plain kosher salt.

makes 4 nonalcoholic cocktails

- 3 pounds peeled seedless watermelon, cut into 1-inch pieces (10 cups), divided
- 2 tablespoons Citrus Rim Salt (page 216) (optional)
- 2 ounces lime juice (2 limes), plus lime wedges for garnishing
- ½–1 ounce Simple Syrup (page 198)
- ¼ teaspoon table salt

1   Spread 5 cups watermelon into single layer on large plate and freeze until firm, about 2 hours.

2   Spread rim salt, if using, into even layer on small saucer. Moisten about ½ inch of 4 chilled collins glass rims by running citrus wedge around outer edge; dry any excess juice with paper towel. Roll moistened rims in salt to coat. Remove any excess salt that falls into glass; set aside.

3   Add remaining 5 cups fresh watermelon, lime juice, simple syrup, and salt to blender and process until smooth, about 30 seconds, scraping down sides of blender jar as needed. Add frozen watermelon and process until smooth, 30 to 60 seconds. Pour into prepared glasses. Garnish with lime wedges and serve.

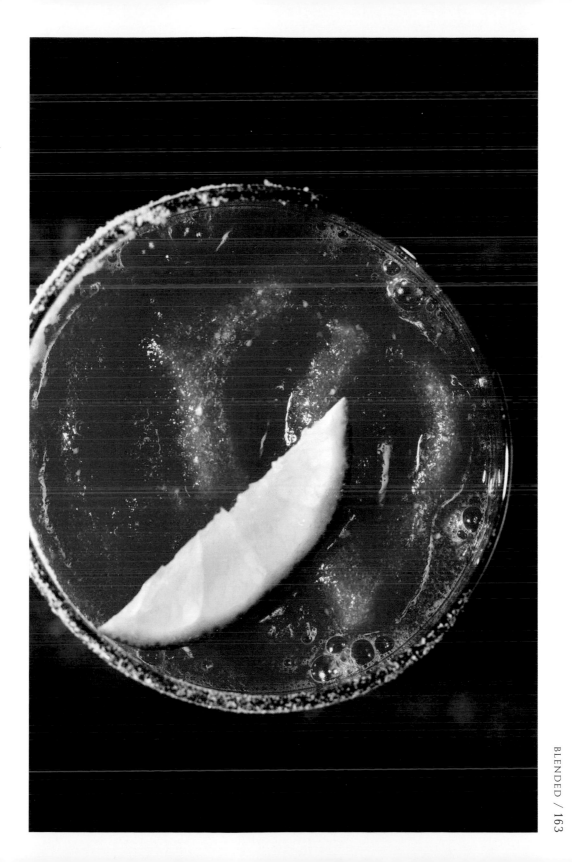

BRANDIED CARAMEL APPLE MILKSHAKES

WHY THIS RECIPE WORKS

Ooey, gooey caramel and sweet-tart apple are a favorite autumn food pairing, but this over-the-top adult milkshake turns the classic flavor combination into a year-round decadent dessert drink. We knew that the subtle flavor of apple could be easily overpowered by the intense caramel, so we used a generous amount of apple butter, which we discovered provided more intense flavor than fresh apples, apple cider, or dried apples. To add the adult kick to this deluxe milkshake, we opted for brandy, which emphasized the sweet, caramelized fruit flavors. A quick whirl in the blender gave this frosty fall-inspired shake an amazingly creamy but sippable texture. Our favorite vanilla ice cream is Turkey Hill Original Vanilla Premium Ice Cream. This recipe can be easily doubled; simply process the milkshakes in two batches. To take this milkshake over the top and really put it into the dessert realm, garnish with whipped cream, a drizzle of caramel sauce, graham cracker crumbs, and apple slices, if you like.

makes 2 milkshakes

- 4 cups vanilla ice cream
- ½ cup apple butter
- 3 ounces brandy
- 2 tablespoons caramel sauce

Let ice cream sit at room temperature to soften slightly, about 15 minutes. Process all ingredients in blender until smooth, about 1 minute, scraping down sides of blender jar as needed. Pour into chilled pint glasses and serve.

ADD A TWIST
Create a nonalcoholic version of these milkshakes by substituting ½ cup whole milk for brandy.

CHOCOLATE-AMARETTO MILKSHAKES

WHY THIS RECIPE WORKS

There are few ice cream treats as nostalgic or as indulgent as a rich and creamy chocolate milkshake, and our amaretto-laced version delivers the goods, packing an intense, chocolaty punch in a decidedly grown-up way. In the test kitchen, we were surprised to find that shakes made with just chocolate ice cream had a certain sourness to them. After some sweet experimentation, we settled on a combination of vanilla ice cream and chocolate ice cream, which gave us the rich chocolate flavor we were after without any distracting sour taste. For an extra burst of deep chocolaty goodness, a little bit of hot fudge sauce went a long way. For our truly over-the-top dessert drink, we loved the way that the amaretto's sweet, nutty flavor lent the shake a brownie-like flavor that was unbeatably delicious. Our favorite vanilla and chocolate ice creams are Turkey Hill Original Vanilla Premium Ice Cream and Turkey Hill Premium Dutch Chocolate Ice Cream. This recipe can be easily doubled; simply process the milkshakes in two batches. To take this milkshake over the top and really put it into the dessert realm, garnish with whipped cream, a drizzle of fudge sauce, and crumbled brownies, if you like.

makes 2 milkshakes

- 2 **cups vanilla ice cream**
- 2 **cups chocolate ice cream**
- 3 **ounces amaretto**
- 2 **tablespoons hot fudge sauce, room temperature**

Let ice cream sit at room temperature to soften slightly, about 15 minutes. Process all ingredients in blender until smooth, about 1 minute, scraping down sides of blender jar as needed. Pour into chilled pint glasses and serve.

ADD A TWIST
Create a nonalcoholic version of these milkshakes by substituting ½ cup whole milk for amaretto.

BIG BATCH

These recipes were created and scaled especially to yield larger batches of cocktails, to serve a crowd at holiday parties, summer barbecues, and more. Most can be made ahead.

CONTENTS

BEST FRESH MARGARITAS

WHY THIS RECIPE WORKS

Margaritas are often thought of as one of the ultimate party drinks, especially the frozen versions. And we won't dissuade you from that notion; we love a well-made frozen margarita as much as anyone (see page 152). However, in a traditional margarita—that is to say, the nonfrozen kind—the fresh citrus flavors have an even stronger chance to shine, as their brightness is not in danger of being dulled by frozen temperatures. For our superior fresh margarita, worthy of being called the best, we sought a balanced blend of fresh citrus flavors and tequila. Mixes and bottled juice had no place in our cocktail. Not only did we insist on freshly squeezed juice, but we also steeped lemon and lime zest in their own juice, along with spirits and Simple Syrup, for a deep, tangy, refreshing flavor. The longer the zest and juice mixture is allowed to steep, the more developed the citrus flavors will be in the finished margaritas. We found that the key was using the right proportions of alcohol and citrus juice—equal parts tequila, orange liqueur, and juice. Blanco tequila will give the margaritas a stronger, more spirit-forward flavor. Reposado tequila, which is aged about 12 months, will bring a smoother, more mellow flavor. For the orange liqueur, you can use a clear-spirit-based one, such as Cointreau; for a richer flavor, try our brandy-based Orange Liqueur (page 228). Feel free to use the Citrus Rim Salt (page 216) or Sriracha Rim Salt (page 217) in place of the kosher salt.

makes 12 cocktails

- 16 ounces blanco or reposado tequila
- 16 ounces orange liqueur
- 4 teaspoons finely grated lime zest plus 8 ounces juice (8 limes), plus lime wedges for garnishing
- 4 teaspoons finely grated lemon zest plus 8 ounces juice (6 lemons)
- 6 ounces water
- 3 ounces Simple Syrup (page 198)
- ½ cup kosher salt (optional)

1 Combine tequila, liqueur, lime zest and juice, lemon zest and juice, water, and simple syrup in bowl. Cover and refrigerate until flavors meld and mixture is well chilled, at least 2 hours or up to 1 day.

2 Strain mixture through fine-mesh strainer set over serving pitcher or large container, pressing on solids to extract as much liquid as possible; discard solids. Keep margarita chilled in refrigerator until ready to serve.

3 Spread salt, if using, into even layer in shallow bowl. Moisten about ½ inch of chilled old-fashioned glass or margarita glass rims by running lime wedge around outer edge; dry any excess juice with paper towel. Roll moistened rims in salt to coat. Remove any excess salt that falls into glass. Serve margaritas in prepared glasses filled with ice, garnishing individual portions with lime wedge.

BLOODY MARYS
FOR A CROWD

WHY THIS RECIPE WORKS

A pitcher of Bloody Marys is a ubiquitous brunch-time classic any time of year. But this is a tricky cocktail to get right. Because vodka is a flavorless spirit, it's easy to add too much, which will put you under the table (faster than you might like). We added varying amounts to the tomato juice and decided that a 3:1 ratio of juice to vodka was the best for both the cocktail's potency and its flavor balance. Another challenge was to balance all the assertive additional flavors: lemon juice, Worcestershire sauce, horseradish, hot sauce, and black pepper. The Worcestershire adds body, depth, and sweetness to a Bloody Mary. We liked a fair amount—more than the dash or two specified in most recipes. And while some Bloody Mary recipes do without grated horse-radish, we loved its robust punch. A little bit, however, goes a long way, so we kept it in check. Tasters were (mostly) in agreement that a Bloody Mary just doesn't taste right without a fairly significant burst of spicy heat. A generous grind of pepper was a step in the right direction, but hot sauce proved a must. We tried a variety of hot sauces in our recipe before deciding on Tabasco for its bright, high heat and galvanizing acidity; you may use another kind if you like, and adjust the amount according to your tastes. We prefer to use Campbell's Tomato Juice in this recipe, though V8 can be substituted. Buy refrigerated prepared horseradish, not the shelf-stable kind, which contains preservatives and additives; do not use horseradish cream. Garnish with pickled green beans, olives, cocktail onions, and/or cornichons in addition to the celery ribs, if desired.

makes 12 cocktails

- 48 ounces tomato juice
- 16 ounces vodka
- 4 ounces lemon juice (3 lemons)
- 1 ounce Worcestershire sauce
- 4 teaspoons prepared horseradish
- 2 teaspoons pepper
- ½–1 teaspoon hot sauce
- 12 celery ribs

1 Whisk tomato juice, vodka, lemon juice, Worcestershire, horseradish, pepper, and hot sauce together in serving pitcher or large container. Cover and refrigerate until flavors meld and mixture is well chilled, at least 2 hours or up to 1 day.

2 Stir Bloody Marys to recombine, then serve in chilled collins glasses filled with ice, garnishing individual portions with celery rib.

CLASSIC SANGRIA

WHY THIS RECIPE WORKS

From its humble—and ancient—roots in Spain, sangria has grown to become a party drink mainstay around the world. Its popularity in the United States dates back to the 1964 World's Fair in New York City. Many people think of sangria as a random collection of fruit chunks in overly sweetened wine. To create a robust, winey sangria with pure flavor, we experimented with untold varieties of fruit and eventually concluded that simpler is better. With red wine, we preferred the straightforward tang of citrus in the form of oranges and lemons, discovering that the zest and pith as well as the fruit itself made an important contribution to flavor. Some orange liqueur complemented and deepened the citrus flavor of the fruit. With white wine, we preferred the crisp taste of apples and pears, highlighted with brandy instead of orange liqueur. For another twist, rosé seemed like a natural pairing with mixed berries; for our liqueur, we wanted something more floral and delicate, and chose elderflower. The longer sangria rests before serving, the smoother and mellower it will taste. Give it an absolute minimum of 2 hours and up to 8 hours if possible.

makes 12 cocktails

- 2 (750-ml) bottles fruity red wine, such as Merlot
- 4 ounces orange liqueur
- 4 ounces Simple Syrup (page 198)
- 3 oranges (2 sliced thin, 1 juiced to yield 4 ounces)
- 2 lemons, sliced thin

1 Combine all ingredients in serving pitcher or large container. Cover and refrigerate until flavors meld and mixture is well chilled, at least 2 hours or up to 8 hours.

2 Stir sangria to recombine, then serve in chilled wine glasses half-filled with ice, garnishing individual portions with macerated fruit.

ADD A TWIST

Make **WHITE WINE SANGRIA** by substituting a fruity white wine, such as Riesling, for the red wine, brandy for the orange liqueur, 8 ounces of apple juice for the orange juice, and 2 apples or pears, sliced thin, for the orange and lemon slices.

Make **ROSÉ SANGRIA** by substituting a rosé wine for the red wine, elderflower liqueur for the orange liqueur, 8 ounces of pomegranate juice for the orange juice, and 2 cups of mixed berries for the orange and lemon slices.

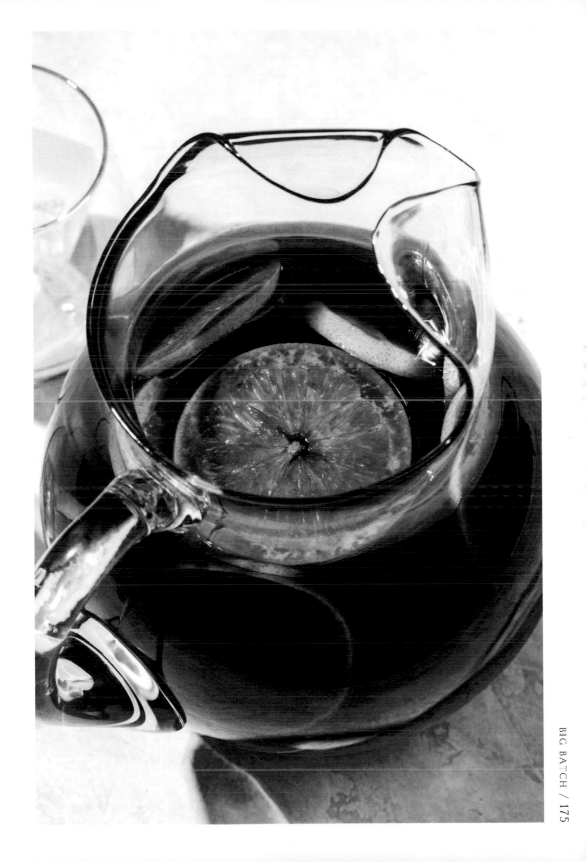

BIG-BATCH
BOULEVARDIERS

WHY THIS RECIPE WORKS

Erskine Gwynne was an American expat of epic reputation across Paris during the 1920s, a bon vivant and man-about-town who founded a literary and cultural magazine called, aptly, *The Boulevardier* (the name means someone who frequents Parisian boulevards). Gwynne is also credited with inventing this deceptively simple cocktail. Depending on its permutation, you could think of the boulevardier as either a bittersweet Manhattan variation or a whiskey Negroni. (Or you could actually think of the Negroni as a boulevardier variation, since the recipe for the boulevardier appeared in print long before the Negroni.) Originally this cocktail called for equal parts bourbon or rye, Campari, and sweet vermouth. However, assertive Campari can be a bully in cocktails, so to keep it under control and prevent it from overwhelming the whiskey, we preferred a smaller ratio of Campari (and vermouth) to the rye. This allowed the drink to walk the fine line between bitter and sweet while maintaining a rich, lush texture. This is a great cocktail to make ahead in a bigger batch because it's both so simple and made up of spirits; there is no citrus juice to develop off-flavors or bitterness by sitting in the refrigerator for an extended period of time. What's more, the measured added water means that you don't even need to add ice cubes before serving. The water ensures the perfect amount of dilution so that you can serve this cocktail straight up to your guests, right from the fridge.

makes 8 cocktails

12 ounces rye or bourbon
8 ounces Campari
8 ounces sweet vermouth
8 ounces water
   Orange twists

1   Combine rye, Campari, vermouth, and water in serving pitcher or large container. Cover and refrigerate until well chilled, at least 2 hours.

2   Stir cocktail to recombine, then serve in chilled cocktail glasses, garnishing individual portions with orange twist. (Big-Batch Boulevardiers may be refrigerated for up to 1 month.)

PIMM'S CUPS

WHY THIS RECIPE WORKS

No drink is more evocative of English summertime than a Pimm's cup. In summer, go to any society event or even a regular pub and ask for one and they'll know exactly what you're talking about (they'll probably have premixed pitchers waiting). Fruit cups were a Victorian homemade concoction of fruit, liqueurs, and gin, and James Pimm is largely credited with making premixed fruit cups popular by serving them at his fashionable oyster bar in the City of London in the 1840s. By 1865, his aperitif known as Pimm's No.1—a gin-based liqueur with sweet fruit and slightly bitter herbal flavors—was sold prebottled, and now "Pimm's" is synonymous with fruit cups. A Pimm's cup is made by combining Pimm's No.1 with English-style lemonade (which is clear and sparkling, with a well-judged sweet-sour balance). It should always be lavishly garnished with fruit. The closest substitute for the lemonade we could find in the United States was lemon-lime soda or ginger ale, but neither passed muster, as both distracted from the spiced, caramelized orange flavor of the Pimm's. Making our own lemonade from Simple Syrup, fresh lemon juice, and seltzer gave us much better results—clean, balanced, and bright. We infused our Pimm's mixture in a pitcher with some fresh lemon slices, cucumber, and mint, garnishing each drink with more of the same. In order to keep the drink sparkling, we gently stirred in the seltzer just before serving. The strawberry is a traditional (and properly British) garnish.

makes 12 cocktails

- 20 ounces Pimm's No.1
- 8 ounces Simple Syrup (page 198)
- 5 lemons (1 sliced thin, 4 juiced to yield 6 ounces), plus lemon slices for garnishing
- 1 English cucumber, sliced thin, divided
- ½ cup fresh mint leaves, chopped, plus mint sprigs for garnishing
- 32 ounces seltzer, chilled
  Strawberries

1 Combine Pimm's, simple syrup, lemon slices and juice, half of cucumber, and mint in serving pitcher or large container. Cover and refrigerate until flavors meld and mixture is well chilled, at least 2 hours or up to 8 hours.

2 Gently stir seltzer into Pimm's mixture. Serve in chilled collins glasses filled with ice, garnishing individual portions with extra lemon slice, remaining cucumber slices, mint sprig, and strawberry.

HIBISCUS-GUAVA AGUA FRESCA

WHY THIS RECIPE WORKS

A popular herbal drink, hibiscus tea is actually an infusion made from the deep magenta-colored calyxes (outer layers) of the roselle flower, a particular species of hibiscus. It has a tart, cranberry-like flavor and is used in many different herbal tea blends as well as on its own. Our goal here was a fruity, refreshing nonalcoholic cocktail that would go down easy at an outdoor party on a hot summer day. To this end, we started by brewing hibiscus tea using our favorite room-temperature brewing method for iced tea. We then sampled our hibiscus tea mixed with every variety of fruit juice we could imagine—including passion fruit, orange, pineapple, and pear—and settled on the sweet, mildly tart taste of guava nectar as the winner. To sweeten our juicy, eye-poppingly pink tea, we favored mint syrup, which brought an herbal lift to the flavor. You could also try Herb Syrup made with basil, tarragon, or thyme in this drink instead of the mint (page 198), or try the Ginger Syrup (page 208). A small dose of lemon juice added some citrus acidity to round out the flavors perfectly and make it even more refreshing after a long afternoon in the sun. For the best flavor, look for hibiscus tea that is 100 percent hibiscus. You can find guava nectar in the international aisle of most well-stocked super-markets; if not, you can substitute pineapple or mango juice.

makes 8 nonalcoholic cocktails

- 10 hibiscus tea bags
- 28 ounces water, room temperature
- 14 ounces guava nectar, chilled
- 4 ounces Herb Syrup with mint (page 198)
- 2 ounces lemon juice, plus lemon slices for garnishing
- ¼ cup fresh mint leaves

1 Tie strings of tea bags together (for easy removal) and place in serving pitcher or large container along with water; let steep for 45 minutes. Discard tea bags. Stir guava nectar, herb syrup, and lemon juice into tea. Cover and refrigerate until well chilled, at least 2 hours or up to 1 day.

2 Stir agua fresca to recombine, then serve in chilled collins glasses filled with ice, garnishing individual portions with lemon slice and mint leaves.

SWITCHEL

WHY THIS RECIPE WORKS

From the 1700s all the way through the 1900s, switchel was traditionally served to farmers working in the fields during haying season. (In fact, another common name for switchel was haymaker's punch.) Today it is still served in some Amish communities. This drink was all about quenching thirst and fortifying the body for more work. You could consider it the original energy drink or health tonic, since both cider vinegar and maple syrup contain potassium, an electrolyte, and ginger contains curcumin, which is an anti-inflammatory. The added ginger was also a way to quell any stomach issues that might emerge as farmers drank so much water in the fields. The vinegar helped to maintain the balance of acidity already present in the body. We liked a balance of 6 ounces cider vinegar to 4 ounces pure maple syrup. Two tablespoons of grated fresh ginger gave the spicy warmth we were looking for without overpowering the delicate maple flavor. Last but not least, the oats gave the drink body. Traditionally, when oats were added, they would not be strained out, and farmers would snack on their switchel soaked oatmeal. The longer you let the switchel chill before straining, the stronger the ginger flavor will be. Do not substitute pancake syrup for the maple syrup. Feel free to adjust the tartness with water to suit your taste.

makes 12 nonalcoholic cocktails

48 ounces water
6 ounces cider vinegar
4 ounces pure maple syrup
¼ cup old-fashioned rolled oats
2 tablespoons grated fresh ginger
1 teaspoon grated lemon zest, plus lemon slices for garnishing
¼ teaspoon table salt

1 Bring all ingredients to brief simmer in large saucepan over medium-high heat. Let cool to room temperature, about 1 hour. Transfer switchel to bowl, cover, and refrigerate until flavors meld, at least 6 hours or up to 1 day.

2 Strain mixture through fine-mesh strainer set over serving pitcher or large container, pressing on solids to extract as much liquid as possible; discard solids. Serve in chilled old-fashioned glasses or mason jars filled with ice, garnishing individual portions with lemon slice.

HOUSE PUNCH

WHY THIS RECIPE WORKS

This sweet-sour punch, with its nutty, spiced flavor undertones, is our more sophisticated take on the zombie cocktail. One of the original tiki drinks, the zombie was invented in Hollywood in the 1930s by Donn Beach at his birthplace restaurant of tiki culture, Don the Beachcomber's. In a clever bit of marketing, Donn imposed a two-per-person limit on ordering the drink, "for your own safety." Nowadays this "lethal libation" is firmly part of the classic tiki drink canon and is a mainstay at most modern tiki bars. Traditionally it's a potent mix of different rums, citrus and other juices, and sweetener. But like many tiki drinks, the recipe has been interpreted badly over the years and has often ended up being a kitchen-sink amalgamation of whatever the barkeep has on hand. Possibly this has led to the more imaginative tales about its madness-inducing properties. While we can't claim ours to be mind-altering, the smooth aged rum, combined with just two juices, nutty orgeat, and warmly spiced syrup, ensured that this drink does go down easy. We prefer to use our homemade Orgeat Syrup (page 202) here; however, store-bought orgeat will work. Freshly grated nutmeg will be the more aromatic and flavorful choice, but preground nutmeg will also work. Fresh pineapple wedges make a nice additional garnish, if you like.

makes 8 cocktails

- 16 ounces aged rum
- 6 ounces pineapple juice
- 6 ounces lime juice (6 limes)
- 4 ounces orgeat syrup
- 3 ounces Spiced Syrup (page 199)
- 1 teaspoon old-fashioned aromatic bitters
  Ground nutmeg

1   Combine rum, pineapple juice, lime juice, orgeat syrup, Spiced Syrup, and bitters in serving pitcher or large container. Cover and refrigerate until well chilled, at least 2 hours or up to 3 days.

2   Stir punch to recombine. Serve in chilled old-fashioned glasses or tiki cups half-filled with ice or containing 1 large ice cube, sprinkling individual portions with nutmeg.

MILK PUNCH

WHY THIS RECIPE WORKS

Don't be fooled by the name of this recipe—it's not milky and creamy like a White Russian. Rather, it's silky-textured and clear, with mellow, harmonious flavors. This is what's often called English milk punch or clarified milk punch. (A creamy and opaque version of this cocktail, called brandy milk punch or bourbon milk punch, is popular in New Orleans.) Clarified milk punch goes all the way back to 17th-century England and was a way to make larger batches of alcoholic mixed drinks that could be stored for extended periods of time without refrigeration. Benjamin Franklin had his own recipe, and bottles were discovered in Charles Dickens's cellar upon his death. What does this mean for the modern home bartender? It means that our Milk Punch is a great make-ahead recipe for entertaining. The base recipe for English milk punch includes citrus juice or another acidic ingredient. Milk is added to the mixed cocktail; the milk curdles in the presence of the acidic ingredients, and then the punch is strained to remove the curds. The process clarifies the drink and preserves it from spoilage. In classic English form, milk punch combines both rum and brandy with a dark beer, like porter or stout, and sugar. This sounds like it might be a rough drink, but the clarification process smooths out and softens any rough edges to bring all the elements into balance. The draining process in step 2 takes about 4 hours to complete but is necessary in order to get the clearest punch possible. Avoid trying to speed up the process by pressing on the liquid in the filter. For an accurate measurement of boiling water, bring a full kettle of water to a boil and then measure out the desired amount.

makes 12 cocktails

- 15 (3-inch) strips lemon zest plus 6 ounces juice (4 lemons)
- 8 ounces Citrus Syrup with lemon (page 199)
- 22 ounces aged rum
- 16 ounces boiling water
- 10 ounces brandy
- 6 ounces porter or stout beer
- 2 cups whole milk

1 Add lemon zest and citrus syrup to large bowl and muddle until fragrant, about 30 seconds. Stir in rum, boiling water, brandy, beer, and lemon juice, then gently stir in milk until curds form. Cover and refrigerate until flavors meld, at least 2 hours or up to 1 day.

2 Line fine-mesh strainer with double-layer of coffee filters and set over serving pitcher or large container. Working in batches, gently pour rum-milk mixture into prepared strainer and let drain completely; discard solids. Cover punch and refrigerate until well chilled, about 1 hour. Serve in chilled cocktail or cordial glasses. (Milk Punch may be refrigerated for up to 1 month.)

HOLIDAY PUNCH

WHY THIS RECIPE WORKS

When the holidays roll around, having a sophisticated, elegant party punch recipe that serves a lot of people is crucial. Champagne punches are truly a classic cocktail category, dating all the way back to the 1700s in Europe. As you might expect with such a long history, there are as many recipes for this cocktail as there are stars in the sky. Unfortunately, most of them are kitchen sink–type recipes, dumping whatever is left over from the holidays into a bowl, with typically disastrous results. For our punch, we wanted a clean, simple recipe with a bit of sweetness but without too much muddled flavor. For a neutral yet flavorful juice, we chose white grape. Our Fruits of the Forest Liqueur gave this drink a deep, mysterious berry flavor as well as a pretty color. A hint of orange liqueur rounded out the fruity sweetness. We preferred prosecco or cava in developing this recipe, but you can use champagne instead, if you like. If you plan to let the punch sit in the bowl for longer than 30 minutes, we recommend adding six large (2-inch) ice cubes to the bowl to keep it properly chilled.

makes 16 cocktails

- 3 (750-ml) bottles dry sparkling wine, such as prosecco or cava, chilled
- 12 ounces white grape juice, chilled
- 6 ounces Fruits of the Forest Liqueur (page 231)
- 6 ounces orange liqueur
- 5 ounces (1 cup) blackberries, blueberries, and/or raspberries
- 5 ounces strawberries, hulled and quartered (1 cup)
- ½ cup fresh mint leaves

Combine all ingredients in large punch bowl. Serve in chilled old-fashioned glasses or punch cups.

EGGNOG

WHY THIS RECIPE WORKS

Winter activities practically demand eggnog, whether it's served to enliven a holiday party or it's ladled out to fortify and warm you up after skiing or snowboarding—or maybe it's simply a reward for getting out there and shoveling snow. Eggnog became associated with the holiday season only after it came to America in the 1700s. Previously it was a drink enjoyed by English monks and upper classes as far back as the 13th century. Today's grocery-store eggnog is often pumped full of sugar and artificial thickeners and stabilizers, and it contains very little actual egg. Our ideal homemade nog is creamy (but not too heavy), just a touch sweet, and fortified with a light but definite note of spirits. Cooking our eggnog resulted in a velvety texture and put to rest any safety concerns about serving uncooked eggs. Opting for heavy cream to replace some of the milk, and whipping half of it before adding it to the eggnog, made for a richer sip. Eggnog can tolerate a variety of brown spirits, including rum, brandy or cognac, or bourbon or other whiskeys. Rum was our tasters' pick over brandy or bourbon: A half a cup packed a punch without over-whelming the other flavors. We preferred black rum, such as Gosling's Black Seal, in our nog. Freshly grated nutmeg is best, but preground nutmeg will also work.

24 ounces whole milk

¼ teaspoon table salt

12 ounces heavy cream

6 large egg yolks

6 tablespoons sugar

4 ounces black rum

¼ teaspoon ground nutmeg, plus extra for garnishing

1   Bring milk and salt to simmer in medium saucepan over medium-high heat, stirring occasionally. Whisk 6 ounces cream, egg yolks, and sugar in medium bowl until thoroughly combined and pale yellow, about 30 seconds.

2   Fill large bowl halfway with ice and water. Slowly whisk 1 cup of warm milk mixture into yolk mixture to temper, then slowly whisk tempered yolk mixture into remaining milk mixture in saucepan. Cook over medium-low heat, whisking constantly, until eggnog registers 160 degrees, 1 to 2 minutes.

3   Immediately pour eggnog into clean medium bowl and stir in rum and nutmeg. Set bowl with eggnog into prepared ice bath and let sit, stirring occasionally, until chilled to room temperature, about 30 minutes. Remove eggnog from ice bath, cover, and refrigerate until well chilled, at least 2 hours or up to 1 day.

4   Just before serving, using stand mixer fitted with whisk attachment, whip remaining 6 ounces cream on medium-low speed until foamy, about 1 minute. Increase speed to high and whip until soft peaks form, 1 to 3 minutes. Whisk whipped cream into chilled eggnog. Serve in chilled old-fashioned glasses or punch cups, sprinkling individual portions with extra nutmeg.

BRANDIED MULLED CIDER

WHY THIS RECIPE WORKS

Bubbling away on the stovetop, mulled cider has a fantastic aroma. Our version tastes even better than it smells, with the rounded, sweet-and-tart apple flavor prominent, complemented by brandy, brown sugar, and spices. After choosing spices for the initial round of testing, one thing became clear: Less is more. The recipes that called for packing the whole spice cabinet into the pot produced harsh, unpleasant cider. We preferred the batches with fewer spices, in which the flavors of each—and that of the apple cider—came through clearly. Before we ruled out any spice or flavoring, we wanted to see if ground or whole spices would work best. We made a batch using each and let them simmer for nearly an hour, standard procedure in many mulled cider recipes. The results were immediately evident. The ground spices floated on top of the cider, making each sip gritty and chalky. We prepared our mulled cider with whole and cracked spices, toasting them briefly for more intense taste. It took only a minute or three extra, and the effort was well worth it. To crack the spices, rock the bottom edge of a skillet over them on a cutting board until they crack. This recipe can easily be doubled. Kept covered in the saucepan, the mulled cider will stay warm for about 30 minutes. The amount of brown sugar will vary depending on the sweetness of the apple cider; start with the lesser amount and add more as needed. Feel free to substitute bourbon or aged rum for the brandy. Cinnamon sticks and apple slices also make great garnishes.

makes 12 cocktails

- 1 cinnamon stick, broken into pieces
- ½ teaspoon black peppercorns, cracked
- ½ teaspoon coriander seeds, cracked
- 7 whole cloves
- 2 quarts apple cider
- 4 (3-inch) strips orange zest, plus orange slices for garnishing
- 1-3 tablespoons packed brown sugar
- 16 ounces brandy

1   Toast cinnamon stick pieces, peppercorns, coriander seeds, and cloves in large saucepan over medium heat, shaking saucepan occasionally, until fragrant, 1 to 3 minutes. Add cider, orange zest, and sugar. Bring to simmer and cook until flavors meld, about 30 minutes, using wide, shallow spoon to skim off any foam that rises to surface.

2   Line fine-mesh strainer with coffee filter and set over large bowl. Strain cider mixture through prepared strainer; discard solids. Return cider mixture to now-empty saucepan and stir in brandy. (Mulled cider can be refrigerated for up to 1 week; bring to brief simmer before serving.) Serve in warmed mugs, garnishing individual portions with orange slice.

MULLED WINE

WHY THIS RECIPE WORKS

Mulled wine is one of the oldest alcoholic mixed drinks, dating back to the ancient Greeks. Roman soldiers in the 2nd century used to heat their wine to fortify themselves against the cold winters, adding sweeteners and other ingredients to make poorly made wine taste better. As they conquered territory and enlarged their empire, the tradition of mulled wine spread. Bad versions of mulled red wine can be reminiscent of cough syrup sickeningly sweet and overspiced, with a harsh taste of alcohol. We wanted to create a warm, not-too-sweet wine with a mild alcohol kick, deep but not overwhelming spice notes, and some fruitiness. For full, round flavors, we chose a careful balance of cinnamon sticks, cloves, peppercorns, and allspice berries, then toasted the spices to unlock their full flavor. We simmered, rather than boiled, the wine, spices, and a modest amount of sugar for a full hour to ensure a full flavored drink that didn't taste raw. A couple of spoonfuls of brandy stirred in just before serving added a fresh, boozy kick. Kept covered in the saucepan, the mulled wine will stay warm for about 30 minutes. Any medium- to full-bodied wine, such as Pinot Noir, Côtes du Rhône, or Merlot, will work well. Extra cinnamon sticks also make great garnishes, if you like.

makes 8 cocktails

- 3 cinnamon sticks, broken into pieces
- 10 whole cloves
- 1 teaspoon allspice berries, cracked
- ½ teaspoon black peppercorns, cracked
- 2 (750-ml) bottles red wine
- ½ cup sugar, plus extra for seasoning
- 4 (3-inch) strips orange zest, plus orange slices for garnishing
- 2 ounces brandy

1 Toast cinnamon stick pieces, cloves, allspice berries, and peppercorns in large saucepan over medium heat, shaking saucepan occasionally, until fragrant, 1 to 3 minutes. Add wine, sugar, and orange zest and bring to simmer. Reduce heat to low and partially cover. Simmer gently, stirring occasionally, until flavors meld, about 1 hour.

2 Line fine-mesh strainer with coffee filter and set over large bowl. Strain wine mixture through prepared strainer; discard solids. Return wine mixture to now-empty saucepan, stir in brandy, and season with extra sugar to taste. (Mulled wine can be refrigerated for up to 1 week; bring to brief simmer before serving.) Serve in warmed mugs, garnishing individual portions with orange slice.

SYRUPS, SHRUBS, BITTERS, AND GARNISHES

Elevating and enhancing your home bar with these recipes for DIY cocktail essentials and accessories will let you take your cocktails to a higher level.

CONTENTS

ESSENTIAL SYRUPS

WHY THIS RECIPE WORKS

Sugar in some form is a fundamental building block of cocktails; the earliest cocktail recipes called for four essential ingredients: spirits, bitters, water, and sugar. Sometimes sugar is used to provide an unequivocal punch of sweetness; other times, it is a single note in a chord of flavors, used to balance acidic, bitter, savory, or other qualities of a cocktail. Modern cocktail recipes sometimes call for granulated sugar or sugar cubes, but these can be difficult to dissolve, leaving you with grit in your drink. Alternatively, some recipes call for sugar in the form of a syrup, usually either simple syrup (with a 1:1 ratio of sugar to water) or rich syrup (with a 2:1 ratio of sugar to water), which is easy to incorporate into all types of cocktails. We wanted to keep things simple (literally), so we came up with a quick method using warm water (no cooking required) to produce a basic simple syrup that we could use in all our cocktails. We developed several flavored syrups by adding herbs, citrus zest, or spices to hot syrup to impart their flavors during the time it took for the syrup to cool. Herb Syrup adds savory notes to the Highlander (page 88) and the Grapefruit-Rosemary Spritzer (page 138). The Spiced Syrup adds warm flavors to the Fireside (page 63). When using these syrups in our recipes, we were careful to account for their specific level of sweetness, as well as their water amount (which affects a cocktail's dilution), in order to achieve perfectly balanced cocktails. These syrups can be refrigerated for up to 1 month. Shake well before using.

SIMPLE SYRUP
makes about 8 ounces

- ¾ cup sugar
- 5 ounces warm tap water

Whisk sugar and warm water together in bowl until sugar has dissolved. Let cool completely, about 10 minutes, before transferring to airtight container.

HERB SYRUP
makes about 8 ounces

- ¾ cup sugar
- 5 ounces water
- ½ cup fresh herb leaves (basil, dill, mint, or tarragon), 12 fresh thyme sprigs, or 1 fresh rosemary sprig

Heat sugar and water in small saucepan over medium heat, whisking often, until sugar has dissolved, about 5 minutes; do not boil. Stir in herb and let cool completely, about 30 minutes. Strain syrup through fine-mesh strainer into airtight container; discard solids.

CITRUS SYRUP
makes about 8 ounces

- ¾ **cup sugar**
- 5 **ounces water**
- 2 **teaspoons grated grapefruit, lemon, lime, or orange zest**

Heat sugar, water, and zest in small saucepan over medium heat, whisking often, until sugar has dissolved, about 5 minutes; do not boil. Let cool completely, about 30 minutes. Strain syrup through fine-mesh strainer into airtight container; discard solids.

SPICED SYRUP
makes about 8 ounces

- ¾ **cup sugar**
- 5 **ounces water**
- 1 **cinnamon stick**
- 8 **allspice berries, lightly crushed**
- 4 **whole cloves**

Heat sugar, water, cinnamon stick, allspice berries, and cloves in small saucepan over medium heat, whisking often, until sugar has dissolved, about 5 minutes; do not boil. Let cool completely, about 30 minutes. Strain syrup through fine-mesh strainer into airtight container; discard solids.

GRENADINE

WHY THIS RECIPE WORKS

A sweet-tart garnet-colored syrup that gives so many cocktails a bright punch of flavor and an unmistakable hue (including the Ombré Sling, page 103; the Frozen Hurricane, page 159; and the Scorpion Cup, page 98), grenadine started appearing in published drink recipes around the turn of the 20th century. Deriving its name from *grenade*, the French word for pomegranate, this sweet syrup traditionally is made from the juice of pomegranates (sometimes with the addition of orange blossom or rose water). Perhaps owing to the high price of pomegranates, some formulas over the years listed cherry or other red fruit juices instead of pomegranate. And over time, as with so many products that have become commercialized, many popular brands did away with natural fruit juices altogether. One of the most ubiquitous current commercial brands lists only high-fructose corn syrup, preservatives, natural and artificial flavors, and artificial colors on its label. There are an increasing number of more authentic grenadine syrups on the market, but they are expensive. We did some calculations and confirmed that making our own traditional version would be not only cost-effective, but also far more flavorful. Using our Simple Syrup (page 198) ratio, we substituted pomegranate juice for the water and included a touch of allspice as a warm counterpoint to the bracing character of the juice. We added a small amount of tangy, earthy pomegranate molasses for deeper flavor, but you can omit it.

makes about 8 ounces

- ¾ cup sugar
- 5 ounces unsweetened 100 percent pomegranate juice
- 8 allspice berries, lightly crushed
- ½ teaspoon pomegranate molasses (optional)

Heat sugar, pomegranate juice, allspice berries, and pomegranate molasses, if using, in small saucepan over medium heat, whisking often, until sugar has dissolved, about 5 minutes; do not boil. Let cool completely, about 30 minutes, then strain through fine-mesh strainer into airtight container. (Grenadine can be refrigerated for up to 1 month. Shake gently before using.)

ORGEAT SYRUP

WHY THIS RECIPE WORKS

Orgeat gets its name from the French word for barley, *orge*, which was its original ingredient. (The French pronunciation of orgeat is *OR-zha*, though you will sometimes hear it pronounced *OR-zhat*.) Over time, almonds were added to the mix, and they eventually prevailed over the barley. Today, no matter how you say it, almond-based orgeat syrup is an indispensable ingredient in many tiki cocktails, notably the Mai Tai (page 97) and our Scorpion Cup (page 98). Its creamy texture, nutty flavor, and light perfume add a compelling *je ne sais quoi* element to otherwise straightforward combinations of fruit juices and rum. Store-bought options often taste overwhelmingly of artificial almond extract, while others are cloyingly sweet yet curiously devoid of flavor. We knew that a homemade version, made with just a few ingredients, could be far superior. We started by heating sugar and water in a saucepan until the sugar dissolved, then we added almonds in various forms (raw, skin-on, blanched, toasted, coarsely chopped, finely chopped) before straining them out. Tasters agreed: We achieved the cleanest, most natural almond flavor from blanched toasted almonds. To maximize their surface area (and lessen the time needed to extract their flavor), we finely chopped them in the food processor before adding them to the syrup. We let the mixture sit overnight before straining out the almonds. The resulting syrup was thick, milky, and full of almond flavor. A little orange blossom water (a traditional ingredient) lent an enchanting hint of floral aroma; look for it in the international aisle of well-stocked supermarkets or in Indian or Middle Eastern markets.

makes about 8 ounces

- 5 ounces blanched whole, sliced, or slivered almonds, toasted and cooled
- 1 cup sugar
- 8 ounces water
- ¼ teaspoon orange blossom water

1 Pulse almonds in food processor until finely chopped, about 30 pulses.

2 Heat sugar and water in small saucepan over medium heat, whisking often, until sugar has dissolved, about 5 minutes; do not boil. Off heat, stir in almonds, cover, and let sit at least 12 hours or up to 24 hours.

3 Set fine-mesh strainer over medium bowl and line with triple layer of cheesecloth that overhangs edges. Transfer almond mixture to prepared strainer and let drain until liquid no longer runs freely, about 10 minutes. Pull edges of cheesecloth together to form pouch, then firmly squeeze pouch to extract as much syrup from pulp as possible; discard pulp. Stir in orange blossom water. (Orgeat Syrup can be refrigerated in airtight container for up to 1 month. Shake gently before using.)

SHRUB SYRUPS

WHY THIS RECIPE WORKS

Sweetened vinegar-and-fruit syrups (also some-times called "drinking vinegars"), shrubs are quite trendy now, but this isn't their first cocktail rodeo. Evidence of acidulated fruit beverages around the world goes back centuries; the version popping up in modern American glasses is believed to have evolved from the fruit-and-vinegar preserves of 17th-century England, continued here by colonists as a way to preserve seasonal fruit. Modern bar menus abound with cocktails (which also, confusingly, can be called shrubs) made from these versatile concoctions. We wanted to develop simple recipes that were bursting with clean, bright, tangy fruit flavor. Our shrub syrups can be enjoyed mixed with seltzer for a simple shrub soda (as in the New Englander or the Southerner, page 41), or they can contribute to the nuances of more complex cocktails (as in the Tartbreaker, page 94). For the mixed berries, you can use any combination of berries in addition to the strawberries (we prefer to use at least two), and you can substitute frozen for fresh. For the peach syrup, we preferred frozen peaches over fresh because of their year-round availability and relatively consistent levels of moisture and sweetness. Tasters preferred cider vinegar in the Peach Shrub Syrup, while they preferred the more delicate flavor of white wine vinegar in the Mixed Berry and Cranberry Shrub Syrups. However, you can use either vinegar in all of these recipes. Note that you must refrigerate the fruit for the Mixed Berry Shrub Syrup for 24 hours. Shrub syrups can be stored in an airtight container for up to 1 month. Shake well before using.

MIXED BERRY SHRUB SYRUP
makes about 10 ounces

- 1 cup blueberries, blackberries, or raspberries, chopped
- 1 cup strawberries, hulled and chopped
- 1 cup sugar
- 2 ounces white wine vinegar

1 Toss blueberries and strawberries with sugar in bowl. Cover and refrigerate for 24 hours, stirring occasionally.

2 Strain berry mixture through fine-mesh strainer into medium bowl, pressing on solids to extract as much liquid as possible; discard solids. Whisk in vinegar.

PEACH SHRUB SYRUP
makes about 10 ounces

- 1¾ cups frozen peaches, thawed and chopped
- 1 cup sugar
- 6 ounces water
- 2 ounces cider vinegar

1 Bring peaches, sugar, and water to boil in large saucepan over high heat. Reduce heat to medium-low, cover, and simmer, stir-ring occasionally, until peaches are soft and beginning to break down, about 10 minutes.

2 Remove saucepan from heat and use potato masher to crush peaches until uniform in texture. Strain mixture through fine-mesh strainer into medium bowl, pressing on solids to extract as much liquid as possible; discard solids. Whisk in vinegar.

CRANBERRY SHRUB SYRUP
makes about 8 ounces

- 2 cups fresh or frozen cranberries
- 1 cup sugar
- 6 ounces water
- 1 ounce white wine vinegar

1   Bring cranberries, sugar, and water to boil in large saucepan over high heat. Reduce heat to medium-low, cover, and simmer until cranberries are beginning to break down, about 5 minutes.

2   Remove saucepan from heat and use potato masher to crush cranberries. Set fine-mesh strainer over medium bowl and line with triple layer of cheesecloth that over-hangs edges. Transfer cranberry mixture to prepared strainer and let drain until liquid no longer runs freely and mixture is cool enough to touch, about 30 minutes. Pull edges of cheesecloth together to form pouch, then gently squeeze pouch to extract as much syrup as possible; discard solids. Whisk in vinegar.

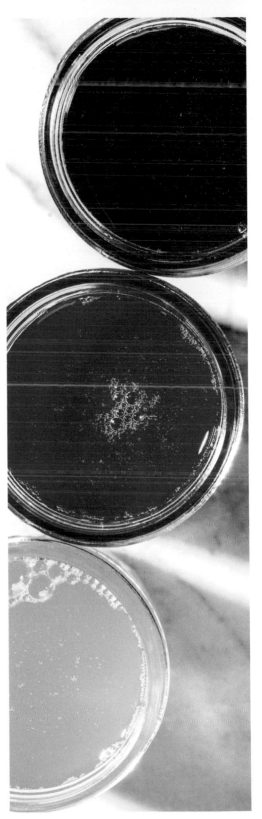

TONIC SYRUP

WHY THIS RECIPE WORKS

If you're a fan of gin and tonics, then you probably know that the tonic water is as important as the gin. Tonic water's characteristic bitterness comes from quinine, an alkaloid extracted from the bark of the tropical cinchona tree. In addition to the many commercial carbonated options, there are also an increasing number of artisanal syrups available for mixing with seltzer to make your own tonic water. We tasted a lineup of nearly a dozen commercially available tonic waters and syrups, and we found they ranged in quality from decent to dismal. Our favorites struck a pleasing balance between bitter and sweet and tended to have bright citrus notes to round them out. We set out to create our own homemade tonic syrup that would rival any store-bought version and could serve as the basis for our very own Favorite Gin and Tonic (page 22). First, we gently simmered cinchona bark, lemon and lime zest and juice, and lemon grass in water for 30 minutes. Next, we added sugar and citric acid (which provides tartness and increases the syrup's shelf life), let the mixture sit overnight to extract as much flavor as possible, and then finally strained out the solids. Unlike commercially produced versions, tonic water made from our syrup has an amber color from the quinine (unless you set it under ultraviolet light, in which case the quinine will fluoresce and appear bright blue!). You can purchase cinchona bark chips online or in specialty spice shops; look for ¼-inch chips. You can purchase food-grade citric acid online or in grocery stores that sell canning supplies.

makes about 16 ounces

- 16 ounces water
- 2 tablespoons (½ ounce) cinchona bark chips
- 5 (3-inch) strips lemon zest plus ½ ounce juice
- 4 (2-inch) strips lime zest plus 1½ teaspoons juice
- 1 lemon grass stalk, trimmed to bottom 6 inches and chopped coarse
  Pinch table salt
- 1 cup sugar
- 2 tablespoons citric acid

1 Bring water, cinchona bark chips, lemon zest and juice, lime zest and juice, lemon grass, and salt to simmer in medium saucepan over medium-high heat. Reduce heat to low, cover, and cook, stirring occasionally, for 30 minutes.

2 Off heat, stir in sugar and citric acid until dissolved. Cover and let sit for at least 12 hours or up to 24 hours.

3 Set fine-mesh strainer over medium bowl and line with triple layer of cheesecloth. Strain syrup through prepared strainer, pressing on solids to extract as much syrup as possible; discard solids. (Tonic Syrup can be refrigerated in airtight container for up to 2 months. Shake gently before using.)

TO MAKE TONIC WATER
Combine 1 part Tonic Syrup with 4 parts chilled seltzer.

GINGER SYRUP

WHY THIS RECIPE WORKS

Truly traditional ginger beer is an alcoholic drink all by itself, a naturally fermented beverage created by a living organism made up of wild yeasts and beneficial bacteria—a sort of ginger beer starter culture. Commercially produced ginger beer today, however, is an entirely different creature: Produced without fermentation, what is called ginger beer under many popular labels is typically a nonalcoholic, slightly more pungent version of ginger ale. When we sampled some of the most popular brands on the market (including those commonly called for in recipes for the most iconic cocktails that contain ginger beer: the Dark and Stormy, page 29, and the Moscow Mule, page 26), we were disillusioned when we read the fine print. Even the ones we thought tasted best contained ingredients we'd rather keep out of our cocktails—high-fructose corn syrup, artificial flavors, and stabilizers. We decided to create a ginger syrup that could serve both as a base for making homemade ginger beer (by combining it with seltzer) and as a vibrant, piquant mixer (by using it in place of simple syrup) in any number of cocktails. As we did when making our Orgeat Syrup (page 202), we started with a basic syrup of sugar and water. We added a hefty amount of chopped fresh ginger plus a touch of ground ginger for extra kick, then we let the mixture sit overnight before straining out the ginger pieces. Finally, a small amount of lemon juice brightened the flavor and increased our Ginger Syrup's shelf life.

makes about 8 ounces

- 8 ounces fresh ginger, unpeeled, chopped coarse
- ¾ cup sugar
- 5 ounces water
- ½ teaspoon ground ginger
- 2 teaspoons lemon juice

1 Process ginger in food processor until finely chopped, about 30 seconds, scraping down sides of bowl as needed.

2 Heat sugar and water in small saucepan over medium heat, whisking often, until sugar has dissolved, about 5 minutes; do not boil. Off heat, stir in chopped ginger and ground ginger and let cool to room temperature, about 30 minutes. Cover and refrigerate for at least 12 hours or up to 24 hours.

3 Set fine-mesh strainer over medium bowl and line with triple layer of cheesecloth that overhangs edges. Transfer ginger mixture to prepared strainer and let drain until liquid no longer runs freely, about 10 minutes. Pull edges of cheesecloth together to form pouch, then firmly squeeze pouch to extract as much syrup from pulp as possible; discard pulp. Stir in lemon juice. (Ginger Syrup can be refrigerated in airtight container for up to 1 month. Shake gently before using.)

TO MAKE GINGER BEER

Combine 1 part Ginger Syrup with 4 parts chilled seltzer.

OLD-FASHIONED AROMATIC BITTERS

WHY THIS RECIPE WORKS

Intensely concentrated botanical elixirs added to cocktails in tiny amounts, bitters have the power to elevate a cocktail to a nuanced, distinctive libation. The world of bitters has exploded, with inventive barkeeps and enterprising amateurs who craft their own versions provoking new appreciation of these potent potions. We set out to create homemade bitters familiar enough to use wherever their commercial counterparts are called for, yet original enough to add distinct character to cocktails. We started by infusing high-proof alcohol (both a solvent and a preservative) with flavoring agents—barks, roots, spices, herbs, flowers, fruits, and nuts—to create dozens of individual tinctures. We combined these tinctures into blends until we settled on one blend —woodsy and earthy, with notes of dried fruit plus just a hint of warm spice—that would be a perfect fit for cocktails such as the Old-Fashioned (page 55), Manhattan (page 50), and New-Fashioned Gin and Tonic (page 66). Then we switched to a straightforward method of combining our flavoring agents in a single jar and covering them with 100-proof vodka; we let the mixture steep for two weeks before straining and sweetening. After fine-tuning combinations, concentrations, infusion times, and sweetener amounts, we had our recipe. If you can't find 100-proof vodka, substitute 80-proof vodka, but add 1 week to the infusion time. We recommend storing your bitters in a cool, dark place to prevent oxidation. Gentian root chips and dried mugwort are bittering agents; you can purchase them, along with dried orange peel, online or in specialty spice shops; look for ¼-inch chips. You will need a quart-size glass jar with a tight-fitting lid for this recipe.

makes about 16 ounces

- ¼ cup raisins, chopped
- 2 tablespoons (½ ounce) dried orange peel
- 2 tablespoons (½ ounce) gentian root chips
- 2 tablespoons dried mugwort
- 8 green cardamom pods
- 10 allspice berries, lightly crushed
- 4 whole cloves
- 16 ounces 100-proof vodka
- 1 ounce Simple Syrup (page 198)

1 Place raisins, orange peel, gentian root chips, mugwort, cardamom pods, allspice berries, and cloves in quart-size glass jar. Add vodka, cover, and shake to combine. Store jar in cool, dark place for 2 weeks, shaking mixture once every other day.

2 Set fine-mesh strainer in medium bowl and line with triple layer of cheesecloth. Strain vodka through prepared strainer, pressing on solids to extract as much liquid as possible; discard solids. Return infused vodka mixture to clean jar and add simple syrup. Cover and shake gently to combine. (Old-Fashioned Aromatic Bitters can be stored in cool, dark place for up to 1 year.)

FRUIT BITTERS

WHY THIS RECIPE WORKS

Once we established our method for making Old-Fashioned Aromatic Bitters (page 210), we returned to our botanical tinctures to explore more fruit-forward blends. To create our superfragrant Citrus Bitters (delicious in the Fireside, page 63, Chancellor, page 74, and Fernet Fizz, page 109), we settled on a combination of fresh sour orange zest (with its exquisitely floral aromas) and lemon. Quassia bark provided the backbone of clean, piney bitterness, and some grassy, lightly floral coriander seeds rounded out the citrus flavors. For our Cherry-Fennel Bitters, we created a base blend of dried cherries and toasted almonds, to which we added a combination of botanicals for character and nuance: vanilla for its slight smokiness, sarsaparilla root for its mild bitterness and licorice and herbal notes, fennel seeds and a bit of star anise for their pungent aromas, dried hibiscus flowers for their floral tartness and gorgeous color, and quassia. We loved these bitters in the Sazerac (page 60) and Amaretto Sour (page 104). Any dried cherries except for unsweetened sour cherries will work. Sour oranges (also known as Seville, bigarade, bitter, or marmalade oranges) can be found in Latin American and Caribbean grocery stores. If you can't find them, substitute the zest of a sweet orange variety (such as navel). If you can't find 100-proof vodka, substitute 80-proof vodka, but add 1 week to the infusion time. You can purchase quassia bark chips, sarsaparilla root chips, and hibiscus flowers online or in specialty spice shops. You will need a quart-size jar with a tight-fitting lid for these recipes.

CITRUS BITTERS
makes about 16 ounces

- 24 (3-inch) strips sour orange zest (3 oranges)
- 8 (3-inch) strips lemon zest
- 2 tablespoons (½ ounce) quassia bark chips
- 1½ teaspoons coriander seeds
- 16 ounces 100-proof vodka
- 2 ounces Simple Syrup (page 198)

1 Place orange zest, lemon zest, quassia bark chips, and coriander seeds in quart-size jar. Add vodka, cover, and shake to combine. Store jar in cool, dark place for 1 week, shaking mixture once every other day.

2 Set fine-mesh strainer in medium bowl and line with triple layer of cheesecloth. Strain vodka through prepared strainer, pressing on solids to extract as much liquid as possible; discard solids. Return infused vodka mixture to clean jar and add syrup. Cover and shake gently to combine. (Citrus Bitters can be stored in refrigerator for up to 1 year.)

CHERRY-FENNEL BITTERS
makes about 16 ounces

- ½ vanilla bean, halved lengthwise
- ¾ cup chopped dried cherries
- ¼ cup slivered almonds, toasted
- 2 tablespoons (½ ounce) sarsaparilla root chips
- 2 tablespoons (½ ounce) quassia bark chips
- 2 teaspoons dried hibiscus flowers
- ½ teaspoon fennel seeds
- ½ star anise pod
- 16 ounces 100-proof vodka
- 1½ ounces Simple Syrup (page 198)

1   Place vanilla bean, cherries, almonds, sarsaparilla root chips, quassia bark chips, hibiscus flowers, fennel seeds, and star anise pod in quart-size glass jar. Add vodka, cover, and shake to combine. Store jar in cool, dark place for 2 weeks, shaking mixture once every other day.

2   Set fine-mesh strainer in medium bowl and line with triple layer of cheesecloth. Strain vodka through prepared strainer, pressing on solids to extract as much liquid as possible; discard solids. Return infused vodka mixture to clean jar and add syrup. Cover and shake gently to combine. (Cherry-Fennel Bitters can be stored in cool, dark place for up to 1 year.)

MASTERING COCKTAIL GARNISHES

When it comes to making cocktails at home, garnishes are often overlooked, skimped on, or simply skipped altogether. But cocktail garnishes should never be an afterthought, because they contribute far more than just decoration to a drink. Cocktail cherries add a slight fruity nuance to a Manhattan (page 50) or an Old-Fashioned (page 55). And it wouldn't be a Mint Julep (page 144) without the effusively aromatic and flavorful mint sprig garnish.

Rimming the outside edge of a serving glass with salt or sugar is an easy and attractive way to intensify the flavor of a cocktail through garnishing. Our Citrus Rim Salt (page 116) tempers the sweetness of the Frozen Margaritas (page 152), and we love our Sidecars (page 83) with a classic sugared rim.

Countless cocktails use citrus zest as a garnish, in one shape or another. Citrus zest is a tool for expressing citrus oil into a cocktail, adding the finishing touch of flavor, aroma, and texture. When we want the lightest touch (as in our Aviation, page 113, where we don't want to overwhelm the delicate floral flavor), we create a narrow coil, simply twisting the zest into a curl over the glass before dropping it in or perching it on the rim. For a stronger burst of bright aroma and flavor, as in our Bichon Frise (page 114), we use a wider strip of peel and pinch it over the top of the drink to express the citrus oils before rubbing the outer edge of the glass with the peel and then dropping it right into the drink.

HOW TO RIM A GLASS WITH SALT (OR SUGAR)

1   Moisten about ½ inch of glass rim by running citrus wedge around outer edge, or by dipping edge of glass in small saucer of water; dry any excess liquid with paper towel. If you prefer, moisten only portion of glass so that you can enjoy cocktail both with and without garnish.

2   Spread ¼ cup kosher salt or sugar (for up to 4 glasses) into even layer on small saucer, then roll moistened rim in salt or sugar to coat. Remove any excess granules that fall into glass.

HOW TO GARNISH WITH CITRUS ZEST

1A   To make citrus zest twist, use channel knife to remove 3- to 4-inch strand, working around circumference of citrus in spiral pattern to ensure continuous piece.

2A   To garnish with citrus twist, curl strand tightly to establish uniform twist, then place in cocktail or on edge of glass.

1B   To make citrus zest peel, use Y-shaped vegetable peeler to remove 2- to 3-inch strip, working from pole to pole and avoiding as much white pith as possible.

2B   To garnish with citrus peel, hold strip horizontal, pith side facing you, near surface of cocktail, with index finger and thumb of each hand. Pinch zest to express oils onto cocktail. Rub outer edge of glass with peel, then place in cocktail.

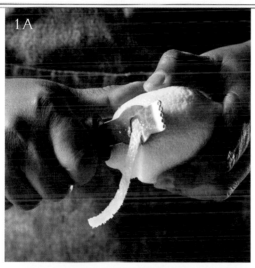

RIM SALTS

WHY THIS RECIPE WORKS

While developing the recipes for the cocktails in this book, we were careful to consider how the specific flavors and qualities of the ingredients could intermingle to craft the most tasteful cocktails. And when we say tasteful, we mean it in the literal sense: We wanted to be sure that the five main tastes—sweet, sour, salty, bitter, and even umami—were deliberately weighed and balanced according to the particular identity of each cocktail. We called upon a range of key ingredients, from syrups, juices, and bitters to eggs, nuts, and dairy products, that helped us add just the right touch of one or another of the tastes we were after to balance the others. We knew that certain cocktails (such as the sweet-tangy Best Fresh Margaritas, page 170, and the savory-spicy Michelada, page 34) sprang to life when we garnished their rims with a bit of salt. But we wanted to take the concept even further, so we developed a series of flavored rim salts that could not only season a cocktail but also add a hint of aroma. We settled on these four. All are quick and easy to make using simple ingredients and your microwave (plus a food processor for the citrus). Do not substitute table or other salts for the kosher salt, as their additives may impart off flavors. See How to Rim a Glass (page 214) for our recommended method for using these rim salts. These rim salts can be stored in an airtight container for up to 1 month. Occasionally they can clump together during storage; break up any clumps before using. These recipes can be easily doubled.

CITRUS RIM SALT
makes about ½ cup

- ½ cup kosher salt
- 1 tablespoon grated lime zest (2 limes), orange zest, lemon zest, or grapefruit zest

Combine salt and zest in bowl, then spread onto large plate. Microwave, stirring occasionally, until zest is dry and no longer clumps, about 2 minutes. Let cool to room temperature, about 15 minutes. Transfer mixture to food processor and pulse until zest is finely ground, 5 to 10 pulses.

HERB RIM SALT
makes about ½ cup

- ½ cup kosher salt
- ½ cup minced fresh basil, dill, or tarragon

Using your hands, rub salt and basil in large bowl until well combined. Spread mixture into even layer on parchment paper–lined rimmed baking sheet. Let sit at room temperature, away from direct sunlight, until completely dry, 36 to 48 hours, stirring every 12 hours to break up any clumps.

SRIRACHA RIM SALT
makes about ½ cup

½ cup kosher salt

⅓ cup sriracha

Combine salt and sriracha in bowl, then spread onto large plate. Microwave, stirring occasionally, until only slightly damp, 6 to 8 minutes. Let cool to room temperature, about 15 minutes. Transfer mixture to food processor and pulse until finely ground, 5 to 10 pulses.

BERRY RIM SALT
makes about ½ cup

You can find freeze-dried berries in the baking or natural foods aisle of most well-stocked supermarkets.

1 cup freeze-dried strawberries, blueberries, or raspberries

½ cup kosher salt

Working in batches, process strawberries in spice grinder until finely ground, about 30 seconds. Transfer to bowl and whisk in salt until combined.

RIM SUGARS

WHY THIS RECIPE WORKS

Sometimes a glimmer of sugar is just what it takes to transform an already delicious cocktail into an elegant, enchanting delight. One impressive way to achieve this is by garnishing the rim of the serving glass with it. For example, although sidecars are often served without sugar rims nowadays, traditionally this cocktail has one, and we loved the extra bit of sweetness it brought to our version (page 83). To avoid creating dessert drinks unintentionally, however, we were careful to call for a sugar rim only for cocktails that were not overly sweet to begin with. To add an even more memorable touch, we developed a trio of scented and flavored rim sugars—Vanilla, Pumpkin Pie Spice, and Smoky Chile—that can be used to add a whiff of aroma or a hint of spice, in addition to sweetness, to complement certain cocktails. (We especially liked the Vanilla Rim Sugar with the Bichon Frise, page 114, the Pumpkin Pie Spice Rim Sugar with the Fireside, page 63, and the Smoky Chile Rim Sugar with the Tumbleweed, page 117.) These mixtures are nothing more than carefully measured amounts of aromatics combined with sugar; they are quick and easy to make and are great to have on hand in your home bar for whenever the mood strikes to put together some extra-special drinks. See How to Rim a Glass (page 214) for our recommended method for applying these rim sugars. These rim sugars can be stored in an airtight container for up to 1 month. Occasionally they can clump together during storage; break up any clumps before using. These recipes can be easily doubled.

VANILLA RIM SUGAR
makes about ½ cup

- 1 **vanilla bean**
- ½ **cup sugar, divided**

Cut vanilla bean in half lengthwise. Using tip of paring knife or spoon, scrape out seeds. Using fingers, rub vanilla seeds and 2 tablespoons sugar together in medium bowl until combined. Whisk in remaining 6 tablespoons sugar. Transfer sugar mixture and spent vanilla bean halves to airtight container and let sit until flavors meld, about 2 days.

PUMPKIN PIE SPICE RIM SUGAR
makes about ½ cup

- ½ **cup sugar, divided**
- 2 **teaspoons ground cinnamon**
- 1 **teaspoon ground ginger**
- ½ **teaspoon ground nutmeg**
- ½ **teaspoon ground allspice**

Whisk all ingredients together in bowl until combined.

SMOKY CHILE RIM SUGAR
makes about ½ cup

- ½ **cup sugar, divided**
- 1 **teaspoon chipotle chile powder**
- ½ **teaspoon smoked paprika**

Whisk all ingredients together in bowl until combined.

COCKTAIL ONIONS

WHY THIS RECIPE WORKS

When brined in a flavorful spiced liquid, mild, naturally sweet pearl onions become the signature garnish for the Gibson (page 48), the pickled onion–lover's riff on the gin martini. Or set out a bowl of them for garnishing when you serve Bloody Marys for a Crowd (page 173), or use them to garnish The Perfect Cheese Plate (page 248). We prefer to use fresh pearl onions for their bright flavor and firm texture and do not recommend using frozen pearl onions in this recipe. Look for fresh pearl onions that are no larger than 1 inch in diameter. Blanching them in boiling water for 1 minute makes it easy to remove their skins. The additives commonly found in table salt (iodine and anticaking agents) can produce off-flavors and hazy brines when making pickles, but canning salt—often called pickling or preserving salt—which is specifically designed for pickle making, doesn't contain additives. This salt also has a very fine grain and dissolves quickly in water. However, you can swap kosher salt for the canning salt: If substituting Morton's Kosher Salt, increase the amount called for here to 2¼ teaspoons; if using Diamond Crystal Kosher Salt, increase the amount to 3 teaspoons. You will need one 1-pint glass jar with a tight-fitting lid for this recipe. Alternatively, you may divide the onions between two 1-cup glass jars.

makes about 2 cups

- 12 ounces small pearl onions
- 4 ounces distilled white vinegar
- 2 ounces dry vermouth
- 1 tablespoon sugar
- 1½ teaspoons canning salt
- 1 teaspoon juniper berries, lightly crushed
- 1 teaspoon coriander seeds
- ½ teaspoon black peppercorns
- 2 (2-inch) strips lemon zest

1   Bring 2 quarts water to boil in large saucepan. Fill large bowl halfway with ice and water. Add onions to boiling water and cook for 1 minute. Drain onions, then transfer to prepared ice bath; drain again. Using paring knife, shave off root ends and tips of onions, then peel off skins.

2   Bring vinegar, 4 ounces water, dry vermouth, sugar, salt, juniper berries, coriander seeds, and peppercorns to boil in now-empty saucepan over medium-high heat, stirring occasionally to dissolve sugar and salt. Add onions, return to simmer, and cook for 2 minutes.

3   Meanwhile, place 1-pint glass jar in separate bowl and place under hot running water until heated through, 1 to 2 minutes; shake dry.

4   Place zest strips into hot jar. Using slotted spoon, pack onions into jar. Using funnel and ladle, pour hot vinegar mixture over onions to cover; you may have some leftover brine. Let jar cool to room temperature, about 30 minutes. Cover and refrigerate for 12 hours before serving. (Cocktail Onions can be refrigerated for up to 2 months.)

COCKTAIL CHERRIES

WHY THIS RECIPE WORKS

The garishly bright-red cherries that garnish everything from ice cream sundaes and fruitcakes to baked hams and cocktails are a far cry from the original maraschino cherry. To make these ersatz maraschinos, sweet cherries are bleached using sulfur dioxide and calcium chloride, then soaked in artificially flavored and dyed sugar syrup. We wanted true maraschinos rather than these chemical bombs. Maraschinos originated in Croatia in the 19th century, when Marasca cherries were preserved in liqueur. This tradition has been preserved most famously (and literally) in Luxardo's Original Maraschino Cherries—rich sour cherries in a velvety syrup—but at over $20 for 14 ounces, we wanted another option: a cost-effective homemade version of luxurious cocktail cherries bathed in an ambrosial syrup. We tested our way through fresh, frozen, jarred, and canned sweet and sour cherries; we preserved them with cherry liqueur, bourbon, brandy, and sugar syrups (including white, brown, Demerara, muscovado, and even caramelized). We hit our sweet (and delicately sour) spot when we soaked jarred sour Morello cherries (similar to but more accessible than Marascas) in a syrup made from unsweetened 100 percent cherry juice and sugar. The key to the syrup was to reduce the juice before adding sugar. We used Trader Joe's Dark Morello Cherries in Light Syrup (available for purchase online) to develop this recipe. You can substitute other jarred or canned cherries; their weight after draining should be 12 ounces. You will need one 1-pint glass jar with a tight-fitting lid for this recipe. Alternatively, you may divide the cherries between two 1-cup glass jars.

makes about 2 cups

- 8 ounces unsweetened 100 percent cherry juice
- 1 cup sugar
- 1 (24.7-oz) jar pitted dark Morello cherries in light syrup, drained

1 Bring cherry juice to simmer in medium saucepan over medium-high heat and cook until juice has reduced to 4 ounces, about 5 minutes. Off heat, whisk in sugar until dissolved.

2 Meanwhile, place 1-pint glass jar in bowl and place under hot running water until heated through, 1 to 2 minutes; shake dry.

3 Using slotted spoon, gently pack cherries into hot jar. Using funnel and ladle, pour hot syrup over cherries to cover; you may have some leftover syrup. Let jar cool to room temperature, about 30 minutes. Cover and refrigerate for 12 hours before serving. (Cocktail Cherries can be refrigerated for up to 2 months.)

PRACTICALLY CLEAR ICE

WHY THIS RECIPE WORKS

You can learn a lot about ice just by looking at it. A pristinely clear cube tells you it's made from pure water in a perfect crystal lattice. Cloudy ice signals impurities, absorbed gases, and irregular crystals. Those impurities (such as chlorine or fluoride) impart unwanted flavors, while absorbed gases (like oxygen and nitrogen) and irregular crystals weaken cubes, making them more prone to shattering while shaking. This creates many unwanted ice shards that will overdilute your cocktail. Bartenders go to obsessive, time-consuming lengths to achieve perfectly clear ice for craft cocktails, but we just wanted an easy at-home technique to get us as close to clear as is practical. We started with distilled water, which cut the impurities to nearly zero. But since air dissolves more readily in cold water, we still had some big bubbles in our ice. By boiling the water and then immediately pouring it into the ice cube tray, most of that air dissipated. The ice still had a hazy center, albeit a smaller one. Insulating the sides and bottom of our ice trays using a baking dish lined with dish towels ensured our ice froze from the top down, pushing trace impurities and air toward the very bottom of our cubes. This left us with 95 percent perfectly clear cubes. We use this method to make 2-inch cubes for serving stirred cocktails and 1-inch cubes for highballs and for shaking. We used our winning brand of silicone ice trays by Tovolo, which measure about 6½ inches by 4½ inches; rubber ice trays also work. If you have larger trays, you may only be able to fit one in the baking dish. You can substitute filtered tap water; however, the ice will not be quite as clear. To remove off odors from silicone ice trays, bake them at 350 degrees for 1 hour.

makes about 7 cups

6 cups distilled water

1 Fold 3 dish towels in half widthwise, then stack in 13 by 9-inch baking dish, allowing towels to overhang edges. Arrange two 6½ by 4½-inch silicone ice cube trays in center of prepared dish. Roll up additional towels and tuck into sides of dish as needed to ensure trays are packed snugly.

2 Bring water to boil in saucepan and let boil for 1 minute. Working in batches, carefully transfer water to 4-cup liquid measuring cup, then pour into trays. Let cool completely, about 30 minutes; you may have extra water. Place baking dish in freezer and let sit, uncovered, until ice is completely frozen, at least 8 hours.

HOMEMADE LIQUEURS AND VERMOUTHS

*These easy-to-make infused liqueurs and vermouths allow you to have
fun with flavors and expand your cocktail-making options. You may even
choose to sip them on their own.*

CONTENTS

ORANGE LIQUEUR

WHY THIS RECIPE WORKS

Orange liqueur is an essential building block for many, many cocktails, from the Sidecar (page 83) to our Best Fresh Margaritas (page 170). You may be more familiar with it by a different name, as this liqueur is known by many labels commercially and has many different formulations. Triple sec and curaçao are generic category examples; Cointreau and Grand Marnier are high-end brand-name examples. We wanted to develop an all-purpose orange liqueur vibrant enough to use wherever such liqueurs are called for in cocktail recipes, but also smooth enough to be enjoyed on its own. Toward this goal, we made batch after batch using various combinations of orange peels and base spirits. We found that a blend of fresh and dried orange peels gave us the most flavorful balance of floral and pungent orange flavors. For the base spirit, we chose brandy for its smooth, well-rounded flavors, rather than a neutral spirit like vodka. Even when made with brandies from the lower end of the price spectrum, tasters deemed these liqueurs far more appealing and sippable than those made with vodka. As you might expect, more mature (read: pricier) brandies yielded a smoother final product, with cognac (a variety of French brandy that can only be made in a certain region) leading the pack. We suggest using a moderately priced brandy that has been aged for at least two and preferably more than four years. You can purchase dried orange peel online or in specialty spice shops; look for pieces that are approximately ¼ inch in size. You will need a pint-size glass jar with a tight-fitting lid for this recipe.

makes about 16 ounces

- 5 (3-inch) strips orange zest
- 1½ teaspoons dried orange peel
- 12 ounces brandy
- 4 ounces Simple Syrup (page 198)

1 Place orange zest, orange peel, and brandy in pint-size glass jar. Cover tightly and shake to combine. Store jar in cool, dark place for 1 week, shaking mixture once every other day.

2 Set fine-mesh strainer in medium bowl and line with triple layer of cheesecloth. Strain brandy mixture through prepared strainer, pressing on solids to extract as much liquid as possible; discard solids. Return infused brandy to clean jar and add simple syrup. Cover and gently shake to combine. (Orange Liqueur can be stored in cool, dark place for up to 1 year. Shake gently before using.)

FRUITS OF THE FOREST LIQUEUR

WHY THIS RECIPE WORKS

Inspired by such iconic berry liqueurs as Chambord (made from black raspberries) and crème de cassis (made from black currants), we set out to create an intensely flavored yet balanced berry-flavored liqueur that could be used whenever these luxurious liqueurs are called for. We started by making batches of liqueurs using the berries we could find most easily at the grocery store: red raspberries, blackberries, blueberries, and strawberries, trying fresh, frozen, and freeze-dried forms of all these berries in our liqueur. Right out of the gate, tasters strongly preferred the bright, intense flavors of the liqueurs made from freeze-dried berries; that they are available in this form year-round was a bonus. And while we loved each of the liqueurs made exclusively from individual berry types almost equally (except for strawberry liqueur, which, on its own, lacked complexity), it was when we combined the flavors that tasters reached consensus. The liqueurs made with combinations of at least two types of berries were bursting with complex, exquisite flavors that were far more interesting than liqueurs made using just any one type of berry. Try this liqueur in the Royal Berry (page 36) and the Holiday Punch (page 189). You will need a pint-size glass jar with a tight-fitting lid for this recipe.

makes about 16 ounces

- 1 ounce freeze-dried blackberries, blueberries, and/or raspberries
- ½ ounce freeze-dried strawberries
- 12 ounces vodka
- 4 ounces Simple Syrup (page 198)

1 Place blackberries, strawberries, and vodka in pint-size glass jar. Cover tightly and shake to combine. Store jar in cool, dark place for 1 week, shaking mixture once every other day.

2 Set fine-mesh strainer in medium bowl and line with triple layer of cheesecloth. Strain vodka mixture through prepared strainer, pressing on solids to extract as much liquid as possible; discard solids. Return infused vodka to clean jar and add simple syrup. Cover and gently shake to combine. (Fruits of the Forest Liqueur can be stored in cool, dark place for up to 1 year. Shake gently before using.)

LIMONCELLO

WHY THIS RECIPE WORKS

Italians often end grand, leisurely meals with a small chilled glass of this refreshing, palate-cleansing liqueur. It also happens to be spectacular in cocktails, such as the Limontini (page 110). Making limoncello is a simple process in which strips of lemon zest are steeped in a neutral spirit to extract flavors and aromas from the zest. Traditionally this takes a month or longer, but we wanted speedier gratification—without compromising flavor—so we turned to the blender. Because alcohol is so efficient at extracting soluble compounds from flavoring agents, we found that processing the zest with vodka in the blender served both to extract these flavor compounds mechanically and to create more surface area on which the alcohol could act to extract flavors more quickly. After just one week, our processed zest yielded as much flavor as strips that had been steeped for a month. To turn this into a popular creamy variation, you can simply substitute half-and-half for most of the water. And to make an orange-scented Arancello, we substituted sour oranges for the lemons. Several varieties (also known as Seville, bigarade, bitter, or marmalade oranges) can usually be found in Latin American and Caribbean grocery stores. If you can't find sour oranges, substitute 20 (3-inch) strips of sweet orange zest (such as navel), 10 (3-inch) strips of lemon zest, and 8 (2-inch) strips of lime zest for the sour orange zest. Over time, a fine sediment (of innocuous pith residue) may form on the surface of the liqueur; if you like, repeat straining through cheesecloth (or simply shake it). You will need a quart-size glass jar with a tight-fitting lid for this recipe.

makes about 32 ounces

- 40 (3-inch) strips lemon zest (4 large lemons)
- 10 ounces vodka
- 1½ cups sugar
- 18 ounces water

1 Process lemon zest and vodka in blender until finely ground, about 30 seconds. Transfer mixture to quart-size glass jar. Cover and store in cool, dark place for 1 week, shaking mixture once every other day.

2 Set fine-mesh strainer in medium bowl and line with triple layer of cheesecloth. Strain vodka mixture through prepared strainer, pressing on solids to extract as much liquid as possible; discard solids. Return infused vodka to clean jar.

3 Heat sugar and water in small saucepan over medium heat, whisking often, until sugar has dissolved, about 5 minutes; do not boil. Let cool completely, about 30 minutes; add to jar with vodka mixture. Cover and gently shake to combine. Refrigerate to chill before serving. (Limoncello can be refrigerated for up to 1 year. Shake gently before using.)

ADD A TWIST

Make **CREMA DI LIMONCELLO** by substituting 16 ounces of half-and-half for 16 ounces of water.

Make **ARANCELLO** by substituting 40 (3-inch) strips of sour orange zest (4 oranges) for the lemon zest.

ANCHO CHILE LIQUEUR

WHY THIS RECIPE WORKS

Fruity, smoky, and mildly spicy, ancho chiles (which are actually dried ripe poblanos) are a natural fit for infusing into tequila. This liqueur works great in our Tumbleweed (page 117), and it also makes a delicious substitute for tequila in our Best Fresh Margaritas (page 170) or other tequila-based cocktails. We found that adding a hint of cinnamon deepened the spicy complexity of the liqueur. The Simple Syrup tempered and balanced the heat of the chiles. As with all of our homemade liqueurs, adding the syrup after the infusion process was complete both avoided diluting the alcohol during extraction and enabled us to have better control over the amount of sweetening in the finished liqueur. We used blanco tequila (white tequila, also known as silver) because of its clean, comparatively neutral flavor and its price point. You can substitute more expensive reposado tequila (rested tequila) or añejo (aged tequila) in this recipe, but we recommend using either of these only if you plan to sip your liqueur on its own (over ice is nice), where its flavors can be fully enjoyed; it's not worth paying the higher price otherwise. Although our favorite base spirit for this liqueur is tequila, vodka or bourbon will also work well. For a spicier liqueur, include the chile seeds when steeping. You will need a pint-size glass jar with a tight-fitting lid for this recipe.

- ½ **dried ancho chile (¼ ounce), stemmed, seeded, and torn into 1-inch pieces**
- ¼ **cinnamon stick**
- 12 **ounces blanco tequila**
- 4 **ounces Simple Syrup (page 198)**

1 Place ancho, cinnamon stick, and tequila in pint-size glass jar. Cover tightly and shake to combine. Store jar in cool, dark place for 1 week, shaking mixture once every other day.

2 Set fine-mesh strainer in medium bowl and line with triple layer of cheesecloth. Strain tequila mixture through prepared strainer, pressing on solids to extract as much liquid as possible; discard solids. Return infused tequila to clean jar and add simple syrup. Cover and gently shake to combine. (Ancho Chile Liqueur can be stored in cool, dark place for up to 1 year. Shake gently before using.)

ADD A TWIST
Make **MOLE CHILE LIQUEUR** by adding ½ teaspoon of cacao nibs and 1 teaspoon of coffee beans to the jar with the ancho chile.

Experiment with flavors by substituting an equal weight of dried guajillo, pasilla, or New Mexico chiles for the ancho.

LAVENDER LIQUEUR

WHY THIS RECIPE WORKS

During the process of researching and developing recipes that call for floral liqueurs, including the Aviation (page 113), which calls for violet liqueur, and the Bichon Frise (page 114), which calls for elderflower liqueur, we became convinced that we needed to add a homemade floral liqueur to our collection. Dried flowers are easy to work with, they are readily available online and in specialty shops, and they infuse quickly into a spirit. Since elderflower liqueur is somewhat ubiquitous, we decided to focus on more-unsung blossoms. We made many batches of floral liqueurs using a broad selection of dried flowers, and tasters settled on four favorite blossoms, with lavender leading the pack. (We also loved chamomile, jasmine, and rose.) We found that in each case, a single strip of lemon zest balanced these floral fragrances with just a hint of fresh citrus aroma. Tasters enjoyed Lavender Liqueur as an alternative to the crème de violette typically called for in the Aviation. Chamomile Liqueur, when combined with Scotch and a thyme-infused syrup in the Highlander (page 88), made tasters feel like they were in the Scottish heathland. Jasmine Liqueur added its heady aroma to our Kiwi Blossom (page 139). Be sure to use food-grade dried flowers (available online or in specialty spice shops) to make these liqueurs; other types likely have been sprayed with pesticides or treated with chemicals. You will need a pint-size glass jar with a tight-fitting lid for this recipe.

makes about 16 ounces

- ¼ ounce dried lavender flowers
- 1 (3-inch) strip lemon zest
- 14 ounces vodka
- 2 ounces Simple Syrup (page 198)

1 Place flowers, lemon zest, and vodka in pint-size glass jar. Cover tightly and shake to combine. Store jar in cool, dark place for 2 days, shaking mixture occasionally.

2 Set fine-mesh strainer in medium bowl and line with triple layer of cheesecloth. Strain vodka mixture through prepared strainer, pressing on solids to extract as much liquid as possible; discard solids. Return infused vodka to clean jar and add simple syrup. Cover and gently shake to combine. (Lavender Liqueur can be stored in cool, dark place for up to 1 year. Shake gently before using.)

ADD A TWIST

Make **CHAMOMILE LIQUEUR, JASMINE LIQUEUR,** or **ROSE LIQUEUR** by substituting dried chamomile flowers, jasmine flowers, or rose petals, respectively, for the lavender.

TEA LIQUEUR

WHY THIS RECIPE WORKS

As with flowers, the flavor compounds of delicate leaves extract easily into alcohol, so it seemed logical to add tea liqueur to our growing array. While the term "tea" is loosely used to describe infusions made from a range of botanicals (including herbs, flowers, roots, fruits, and others), we limited ours to true tea: the cured leaves of the *Camellia sinensis* bush. Tea leaves are processed in various ways to produce many types of tea. We settled on black and green teas for making our tea liqueurs, as tasters preferred their flavors and they were the most commonly available. Black teas (such as Assam, Ceylon, and Darjeeling, which are sometimes enhanced with additional flavors to make such familiar blends as English breakfast, Irish breakfast, Earl Grey, and masala chai) are made from oxidized tea leaves and are bold, tannic teas. One of our favorite black teas, Lapsang souchong, is smoke-dried, with a unique woodsy-smoky flavor. Green teas are made from unoxidized tea leaves and have bittersweet, grassy notes. They are sometimes enhanced with additional flavor elements (such as roasted popped brown rice to make genmaicha tea). Any of these styles of black or green tea can be used in this recipe. This liqueur can be made overnight, which means that if on Thursday you start making your tea liqueur, by Friday night you could be enjoying a Teatini (page 71) or a Hole in One (page 135). You will need a pint-size glass jar with a tight-fitting lid for this recipe.

makes about 16 ounces

- 1 tablespoon dried black or green tea
- 14 ounces vodka
- 2 ounces Simple Syrup (page 198)

1 Place tea and vodka in pint-size glass jar. Cover tightly and shake to combine. Store jar in cool, dark place for 1 day, shaking mixture occasionally.

2 Set fine-mesh strainer in medium bowl and line with triple layer of cheesecloth. Strain vodka mixture through prepared strainer, pressing on solids to extract as much liquid as possible; discard solids. Return infused vodka to clean jar and add simple syrup. Cover and gently shake to combine. (Tea Liqueur can be stored in cool, dark place for up to 1 year. Shake gently before using.)

COFFEE LIQUEUR

WHY THIS RECIPE WORKS

Rich and earthy, with hints of chocolate, whispers of vanilla, and a trace of toasted nuttiness, this liqueur—whether shaken into an Espresso Martini (page 120), tipped into a cup of hot coffee (or added to Irish Coffee, page 43), served over ice, stirred into cake batter, or drizzled over ice cream—is a coffee lover's perfect buzz. We made different batches of liqueurs using both whole and ground coffee beans that had been roasted to varying degrees. We quickly eliminated ground coffee from the running, as the results were too bitter and cloudy. Some tasters loved the bracing flavor of liqueur made with dark-roast coffee beans, but most preferred the smoother, more balanced flavors of medium-roast beans. After testing different extraction times, we found that infusing the beans in alcohol for one week was all that was necessary to achieve the best flavor; any longer and the flavors verged on sharp and bitter. Next, we added a small amount of cacao nibs and a piece of vanilla bean—just enough to create delicate flavor harmonies. Adding a small amount of brandy to the vodka base contributed lovely caramel and oaky notes. Finally, we made sure to finish it with the right amount of sweetness. For a more intensely flavored liqueur, you can substitute dark-roast coffee beans for the medium-roast; we do not recommend using light-roast beans. You can substitute 1½ teaspoons cocoa powder for the cacao nibs, but the resulting liqueur will be slightly cloudy. You will need a pint-size glass jar with a tight-fitting lid for this recipe.

makes about 16 ounces

- ½ cup medium-roast coffee beans
- 1½ teaspoons cacao nibs
- ¼ vanilla bean, halved lengthwise
- 8 ounces vodka
- 4 ounces brandy
- 4 ounces Simple Syrup (page 198)

1 Place coffee beans, cacao nibs, vanilla bean, vodka, and brandy in pint-size glass jar. Cover tightly and shake to combine. Store jar in cool, dark place for 1 week, shaking mixture once every other day

2 Set fine-mesh strainer in medium bowl and line with triple layer of cheesecloth. Strain vodka mixture through prepared strainer; discard solids. Return infused vodka mixture to clean jar and add simple syrup. Cover and gently shake to combine. (Coffee Liqueur can be stored in cool, dark place for up to 1 year. Shake gently before using.)

DRY VERMOUTH

WHY THIS RECIPE WORKS

Our homemade Dry Vermouth might just make your next Gin Martini (page 48) the best you've ever had. It also makes a stealth appearance in the Scotch-forward Chancellor (page 74). Or for the ultimate vermouth cocktail, try the French Kiss (page 77), which combines equal parts dry and sweet vermouth for an elegant low-alcohol aperitif. Our rendition of dry vermouth is herbal and grassy, its winey acidity balanced by just a touch of Simple Syrup, to take the edge off the bittering agents. Commercial vermouth makers extract botanical flavors using a combination of distillation and maceration. For our version, we wanted great results from a straightforward approach. We tried simmering botanicals in wine, but the heat destroyed some of the delicate flavors. Infusing wine with botanicals at room temperature didn't work either, as the flavors never got beyond tepid. Then we added botanicals to a jar with a small amount of the fortifying spirit; after just 24 hours, the vodka had extracted a complex and vibrant array of aromas. To that base, we added enough wine to achieve the proper level of alcohol by volume. We prefer to use Pinot Grigio (Pinot Gris in French), but you can substitute your favorite unoaked dry white wine. You can purchase dried wormwood, chamomile flowers, and quassia bark chips online or in specialty spice shops; look for chips that are approximately ¼ inch in size. You will need a quart-size glass jar with a tight-fitting lid for this recipe.

makes about 32 ounces

- 6 ounces vodka
- 1 (3-inch) strip orange zest
- 1 bay leaf
- 1 teaspoon dried wormwood
- 1 teaspoon dried chamomile flowers
- 1 teaspoon dried sage
- 6 juniper berries, lightly crushed
- ½ teaspoon coriander seeds
- ½ teaspoon dried thyme
- ¼ teaspoon black peppercorns
- ¼ teaspoon quassia bark chips
- 2 whole cloves
- 1 green cardamom pod
- ½ star anise pod
- 20 ounces Pinot Grigio
- 1½ ounces Simple Syrup (page 198)

1 Combine vodka, orange zest, bay leaf, wormwood, chamomile flowers, sage, juniper berries, coriander seeds, thyme, peppercorns, quassia bark chips, cloves, cardamom pod, and star anise pod in quart-size glass jar. Cover and store jar in cool, dark place for at least 12 hours or up to 24 hours.

2 Set fine-mesh strainer in medium bowl and line with triple layer of cheesecloth. Strain vodka mixture through prepared strainer, pressing on solids to extract as much liquid as possible; discard solids. Return infused vodka to clean jar and add wine and simple syrup. Cover and gently shake to combine. (Dry Vermouth can be refrigerated for up to 3 months. Shake gently before using.)

SWEET VERMOUTH

WHY THIS RECIPE WORKS

Indispensable to the Manhattan (page 50), Negroni (page 59), and Americano (page 30), sweet vermouth plays a special role in defining how good—or how mediocre—these classics can be. In America, the most commonly known sweet vermouths are Italian, but there are also important vermouth traditions in France and in Spain, where *la hora del vermut* ("the hour of vermouth") is essentially a synonym for happy hour. We tasted many commercially produced sweet vermouths; our favorites were at once herbal (redolent of their namesake herb, wormwood, plus notes of sage and thyme), floral, bitter, and warmly spiced. For our homemade version, we used the same basic method as for our Dry Vermouth (page 242), but we added golden raisins for their concentrated fruity sweetness, and we emphasized the warmer spices and floral flavors while keeping the herbal notes in balance. For enriched sweetening and to contribute to the color, we made an easy stovetop caramel syrup, adding it to our mixture of aromatized wine and vodka. The optional hibiscus flowers bring it closer to the garnet shade of commercial vermouths, but they may be omitted. We prefer to use Pinot Grigio (Pinot Gris in French), but you can substitute your favorite unoaked dry white wine. You can purchase dried wormwood, chamomile flowers, hibiscus flowers, and quassia bark chips online or in specialty spice shops; look for chips that are approximately ¼ inch in size. For an accurate measurement of boiling water, bring a full kettle of water to a boil and then measure out the desired amount. You will need a quart-size glass jar with a tight-fitting lid for this recipe.

makes about 32 ounces

- 6 ounces vodka
- ½ cup golden raisins, chopped
- 2 (3-inch) strips orange zest
- 1 bay leaf
- 1 teaspoon dried wormwood
- 1 teaspoon dried chamomile flowers
- 6 juniper berries, lightly crushed
- ½ teaspoon quassia bark chips
- ½ teaspoon coriander seeds
- ½ teaspoon dried sage
- ½ teaspoon dried thyme
- ¼ teaspoon black peppercorns
- 4 whole cloves
- 2 green cardamom pods
- ½ star anise pod
- 2 teaspoons dried hibiscus flowers (optional)
- 6 ounces boiling water, divided
- ¾ cup sugar
- 20 ounces Pinot Grigio

1   Combine vodka, raisins, orange zest, bay leaf, wormwood, chamomile flowers, juniper berries, quassia bark chips, coriander seeds, sage, thyme, peppercorns, cloves, cardamom pods, and star anise pod in quart-size glass jar. Cover and store jar in cool, dark place for at least 12 hours or up to 24 hours.

2   Set fine-mesh strainer in medium bowl and line with triple layer of cheesecloth. Strain vodka mixture through prepared strainer, pressing on solids to extract as much liquid as possible; discard solids. Set aside.

3   If using hibiscus, combine flowers and 4 ounces boiling water in bowl and let steep for 5 minutes. Strain through fine-mesh strainer into separate bowl, pressing on solids to extract as much liquid as possible.

4   Combine sugar and 2 ounces boiling water in medium saucepan. Bring to boil over medium-high heat and cook, without stirring, until mixture is amber-colored around edges of saucepan. Reduce heat to low and continue to cook, swirling saucepan occasionally, until caramel is evenly dark amber, 3 to 5 minutes. Off heat, carefully whisk in either hibiscus tea or remaining 4 ounces boiling water (mixture will bubble and steam) until syrup is smooth. Immediately transfer caramel to large bowl and let cool completely, about 30 minutes.

5   Add infused vodka, wine, and caramel to clean jar, cover, and gently shake to combine. (Sweet Vermouth can be refrigerated for up to 3 months. Shake gently before using.)

NO. 9

SNACKS

*Cocktail hour isn't complete without some equally tempting
accompaniments to spark your thirst. Here are a few of our
simple-yet-sophisticated favorites.*

CONTENTS

THE PERFECT CHEESE PLATE

- Start by choosing three to five cheeses with different textures (soft, semisoft, semifirm, hard) and flavors (mild to strong). Include cow's-milk, goat's-milk, and sheep's-milk cheeses, or go with all of one type. Plan on 2 to 3 ounces of cheese per person and let the cheese sit at room temperature, covered, for 1 to 2 hours before serving.

- Think about breads: Mild-flavored bread such as a baguette and neutral-tasting crackers like water crackers or wheat crackers won't overshadow the cheeses.

- Think about texture: Crisp apple slices and crunchy Spiced Nuts (opposite) can add contrast to soft cheeses. The texture of soft pear slices and chewy dried fruits works with hard cheeses.

- Think about flavor: Select cheese accompaniments that are either complementary, like a mellow caramelized onion relish with a mild fresh cheese, or contrasting, like fruity Fig-Balsamic Jam (opposite) with a salty, sharp aged cheese.

- Think about appearance: Fresh berries, grapes, dried fruits, cornichons and other pickles, and Marinated Olives (page 250) add color as well as texture and flavor.

SPICED NUTS
serves 8

Superior to any store-bought mix, these nuts are an elegant addition to a cheese plate and are also wonderful served on their own. If you can't find superfine sugar, process granulated sugar in a food processor for 1 minute.

- 1 large egg white
- 1 tablespoon water
- 1 teaspoon table salt
- 1 pound pecans, raw cashews, walnuts, or whole unblanched almonds, or a combination
- ⅔ cup superfine sugar
- 2 teaspoons cumin
- 1 teaspoon cayenne pepper
- 1 teaspoon paprika

1 Adjust oven racks to upper-middle and lower-middle positions and heat oven to 275 degrees. Line 2 rimmed baking sheets with parchment paper. Whisk egg white, water, and salt together in medium bowl. Add nuts and toss to coat. Let nuts drain in colander for 5 minutes.

2 Mix sugar, cumin, cayenne, and paprika together in clean medium bowl. Add drained nuts and toss to coat. Spread nuts evenly over prepared baking sheets. Bake until nuts are dry and crisp, about 50 minutes, stirring occasionally. Let nuts cool completely on baking sheets, about 30 minutes. Break nuts apart and serve. (Spiced Nuts can be stored in airtight container for up to 1 week.)

FIG-BALSAMIC JAM
makes about 1 cup

Combining fresh figs with balsamic vinegar and spices makes a sweet-savory jam that's fantastic with cheese. It's also delicious as an accompaniment to canapés, such as crostini draped with prosciutto or spread with pâté.

- 12 ounces fresh figs, stemmed and quartered
- ½ cup sugar
- ¼ cup balsamic vinegar
- ¼ cup water
- 1 tablespoon lemon juice
- 1 teaspoon yellow mustard seeds
- ¾ teaspoon minced fresh rosemary
  Pinch table salt
  Pinch pepper

1 Bring all ingredients to simmer in 10-inch nonstick skillet over medium-high heat. Reduce heat to medium-low and cook, stirring occasionally, until rubber spatula leaves distinct trail when dragged across bottom of skillet, 25 to 30 minutes.

2 Transfer jam to food processor and pulse until uniformly chunky, 4 to 6 pulses. Let jam cool to room temperature, about 1 hour, before serving. (Fig-Balsamic Jam can be refrigerated for up to 2 months.)

BOWLS FOR NIBBLING

MARINATED OLIVES
serves 8

Olives belong in more than just a martini. Set out a bowl of this zesty mix with cocktails that lean toward the savory side.

- 1 cup brine-cured green olives with pits
- 1 cup brine-cured black olives with pits
- ¾ cup extra-virgin olive oil
- 1 shallot, minced
- 2 teaspoons grated lemon zest
- 2 teaspoons minced fresh thyme
- 2 teaspoons minced fresh oregano
- 1 garlic clove, minced
- ½ teaspoon red pepper flakes
- ½ teaspoon table salt

Pat olives dry with paper towels. Toss with oil, shallot, lemon zest, thyme, oregano, garlic, pepper flakes, and salt in bowl. Cover and refrigerate for at least 4 hours or up to 4 days. Let sit at room temperature for at least 30 minutes before serving.

PARMESAN-PEPPER POPCORN
serves 6 to 8

Elevate a perennial party snack with Parmesan and black pepper. Use a 5-quart or larger Dutch oven for popping the corn.

- 2 tablespoons vegetable oil
- ½ cup popcorn kernels
- 1 ounce Parmesan cheese, grated (½ cup)
- 3 tablespoons unsalted butter, melted
- ½ teaspoon pepper
- ¼ teaspoon table salt

Add oil and popcorn to Dutch oven. Cover and cook over medium-high heat, shaking occasionally, until first few kernels begin to pop. Continue to cook, shaking pot vigorously, until popping has mostly stopped. Transfer to large bowl. Toss with Parmesan, melted butter, pepper, and salt. Serve.

ASIAN FIRECRACKER PARTY MIX
serves 10 to 12

Our homemade snack mix is a smash hit, especially with tiki or tropical drinks.

- 5 cups Corn Chex cereal
- 2 cups sesame sticks
- 1 cup wasabi peas
- 1 cup chow mein noodles
- 1 cup honey-roasted peanuts
- 6 tablespoons unsalted butter, melted
- 2 tablespoons soy sauce
- 1 teaspoon ground ginger
- ¾ teaspoon garlic powder
- ¼ teaspoon cayenne pepper

1   Adjust oven rack to middle position and heat oven to 250 degrees. Combine cereal, sesame sticks, peas, chow mein noodles, and peanuts in large bowl. Whisk melted butter, soy sauce, ginger, garlic powder, and cayenne together in separate bowl, then drizzle over cereal mixture and toss until well combined.

2   Spread mixture on rimmed baking sheet and bake, stirring every 15 minutes, until golden and crisp, about 45 minutes. Let cool to room temperature before serving.

EVERYONE LOVES DIP

SPICY WHIPPED FETA
serves 8

Serve this tangy, salty, rich dip with pita chips, pita bread, or cucumber spears.

- 1 pound feta cheese, rinsed and patted dry, cut into ½-inch pieces (4 cups)
- ⅓ cup extra-virgin olive oil, plus extra for drizzling
- 1 tablespoon lemon juice
- ¼–½ teaspoon cayenne pepper
- ½ teaspoon pepper

Process all ingredients in food processor until smooth, about 20 seconds, scraping down sides of bowl as needed; transfer to serving bowl. (Dip can be refrigerated for up to 2 days; bring to room temperature.) Drizzle with extra oil before serving.

BACON, SCALLION, AND CARAMELIZED ONION DIP
serves 4 to 6

Pair this modern, grown-up take on onion dip with your fanciest potato chips.

- 3 slices bacon, cut into ¼-inch pieces
- 1½ teaspoons unsalted butter
- 1 pound onions, halved through root end and sliced crosswise ¼ inch thick
- ½ teaspoon light brown sugar
- ¼ teaspoon table salt
- 1½ teaspoons water
- ¾ cup sour cream
- 2 scallions, minced
- ½ teaspoon cider vinegar

1 Cook bacon in 12-inch nonstick skillet over medium heat until crisp, 5 to 7 minutes. Using slotted spoon, transfer bacon to paper towel–lined plate; set aside. Pour off all but 1½ teaspoons fat from skillet.

2 Add butter to fat left in skillet and heat over high heat until melted. Add onions, sugar, and salt and cook, stirring occasionally, until onions begin to soften and release some moisture, about 5 minutes. Reduce heat to medium and continue to cook, stirring frequently, until deeply browned and slightly sticky, about 40 minutes. (If onions are sizzling or scorching, reduce heat. If onions are not browning after 15 to 20 minutes, increase heat.) Off heat, stir in water and season with pepper to taste.

3 Combine sour cream, scallions, vinegar, bacon, and caramelized onions in serving bowl. Season with salt and pepper to taste. Serve. (Dip can be refrigerated for up to 3 days; stir to recombine.)

ROSEMARY AND GARLIC WHITE BEAN DIP
serves 8 to 10

Complementing a wide range of dippers, this cannellini bean dip is a secret party weapon.

- 2 (15-ounce) cans cannellini beans, rinsed
- ½ cup extra-virgin olive oil, divided
- ¼ cup water
- 2 tablespoons lemon juice
- 2 garlic cloves, minced
- ½ teaspoon chopped fresh rosemary

1 Process two-thirds of beans, 6 tablespoons oil, water, lemon juice, garlic, and rosemary in food processor until smooth, about 10 seconds, scraping down sides of bowl as needed. Add remaining beans and pulse just to incorporate. Transfer to serving bowl and let sit at room temperature until flavors meld, at least 30 minutes. (Dip can be refrigerated for up to 4 days; bring to room temperature.)

2 Season dip with salt and pepper to taste. To serve, make small well in center and pour remaining 2 tablespoons oil into well.

HERBED SPINACH DIP
serves 4 to 6

Fresh herbs, garlic, and hot sauce ensure this is no ordinary spinach dip. Serve with crudités.

- 10 ounces frozen chopped spinach, thawed and squeezed dry
- ½ red bell pepper, chopped fine
- ½ cup sour cream
- ½ cup mayonnaise
- ½ cup fresh parsley leaves
- 3 scallions, sliced thin
- 1 tablespoon minced fresh dill
- 1 garlic clove, minced
- ½ teaspoon table salt
- ¼ teaspoon pepper
- ¼ teaspoon hot sauce

Process all ingredients in food processor until well combined, about 1 minute, scraping down sides of bowl as needed. Transfer to serving bowl, cover, and refrigerate until flavors meld, at least 1 hour or up to 3 days. Season with salt and pepper to taste. Serve.

PERFECT FOR PASSING

ASPARAGUS PUFFS
serves 6 to 8

Puff pastry envelops an asparagus and two-cheese filling in these warm baked cocktail poppers. To thaw frozen puff pastry, let sit in the refrigerator for 24 hours or on the counter for 30 minutes to 1 hour.

- 12 ounces asparagus, trimmed
     Table salt for blanching asparagus
- 4 ounces goat cheese, room temperature
- 2 ounces Parmesan cheese, grated (1 cup), divided
- ¼ cup minced fresh chives
- 1 teaspoon grated lemon zest plus 2 teaspoons juice
- 2 (9 ½ by 9-inch) sheets puff pastry, thawed
- 2 large eggs, lightly beaten

1 Adjust oven racks to upper-middle and lower-middle positions and heat oven to 375 degrees. Line 2 rimmed baking sheets with parchment paper. Bring 2½ quarts water to boil in large saucepan. Add asparagus and 1 teaspoon salt and cook until asparagus is bright green and still crisp, about 1 minute. Meanwhile, fill large bowl halfway with ice and water. Drain asparagus, then transfer immediately to ice bath. Let asparagus cool completely, about 5 minutes, then drain, pat dry with paper towels, and chop fine.

2 Combine goat cheese, ¾ cup Parmesan, chives, lemon zest and juice, and asparagus in bowl and season with salt and pepper to taste. (Filling can be refrigerated for up to 1 day.)

3 Unfold both sheets pastry onto lightly floured counter; flatten any creases. Roll each sheet into 12-inch square. Using 3-inch round cookie cutter, cut out 32 circles. Brush circles with egg. Place 2 teaspoons filling slightly off center on each circle. Fold circle over filling and crimp edges with fork to seal.

4 Place puffs on prepared sheets. Brush with remaining egg and sprinkle with remaining ¼ cup Parmesan. Bake until puffed and golden, about 20 minutes, switching and rotating sheets halfway through baking. Let puffs cool on sheets for 5 minutes; serve warm.

PROSCIUTTO-WRAPPED STUFFED DATES
serves 6 to 8

Sweet-salty and irresistible. High-quality, thinly sliced prosciutto is essential here. Look for Medjool dates, as they are particularly sweet, with a dense yet plump texture.

- ⅔ cup walnuts, toasted and chopped fine
- ½ cup minced fresh parsley
- 2 tablespoons extra-virgin olive oil
- ½ teaspoon grated orange zest
- 12 large pitted dates, halved lengthwise
- 12 thin slices prosciutto, halved lengthwise

Combine walnuts, parsley, oil, and orange zest in bowl; season with salt and pepper to taste. Mound 1 generous teaspoon filling into center of each date half. Wrap prosciutto securely around dates. Serve. (Dates can be refrigerated for up to 8 hours; bring to room temperature before serving.)

BRUSCHETTA WITH OLIVE PESTO, RICOTTA, AND BASIL
serves 8 to 10

A piquant olive pesto with shallot, lemon, and garlic tops toasted bread slices. You can make the pesto ahead, but toast the bread just before assembling the bruschetta.

- ½ cup pitted kalamata olives
- 1 small shallot, minced
- ¼ cup extra-virgin olive oil, divided, plus extra for serving
- 1½ teaspoons lemon juice
- 2 garlic cloves (1 minced, 1 whole)
- 1 loaf country bread, ends discarded, sliced crosswise into ¾-inch-thick pieces
- 12 ounces (1½ cups) whole-milk ricotta cheese
- 2 tablespoons shredded fresh basil

1   Process olives, shallot, 2 tablespoons oil, lemon juice, and minced garlic in food processor until uniform paste forms, about 10 seconds, scraping down sides of bowl as needed. (Pesto can be refrigerated for up to 1 day.)

2   Adjust oven rack 4 inches from broiler element and heat broiler. Place bread on aluminum foil–lined rimmed baking sheet. Broil until bread is deep golden on both sides, 1 to 2 minutes per side. Lightly rub 1 side of each slice with whole garlic clove and brush with remaining 2 tablespoons oil. Spread ricotta evenly on toasts, then carefully spread pesto on top. Drizzle with extra oil and sprinkle with basil and salt to taste. Serve.

RESOURCE GUIDE

You can mail-order any of the specialty ingredients in this book from Amazon. Here are some additional sources:

HERBS OF MEXICO
herbsofmexico.com/store

Flowers: chamomile, hibiscus, lavender, and rose petals

Botanicals: cinchona bark chips, gentian root chips, mugwort, quassia bark chips, sarsaparilla root chips, and wormwood

KALUSTYAN'S
foodsofnations.com

Flowers: chamomile, hibiscus, jasmine, lavender, and rose petals

Botanicals: cinchona bark chips, mugwort, quassia bark chips, sarsaparilla root chips, and wormwood

Other ingredients: citric acid

MOUNTAIN ROSE HERBS
mountainroseherbs.com

Flowers: chamomile, hibiscus, and lavender

Botanicals: gentian root chips, mugwort, sarsaparilla root chips, and wormwood

Other ingredients: citric acid

PENN HERB
pennherb.com

Flowers: chamomile, hibiscus, jasmine, lavender, and rose petals

Botanicals: cinchona bark chips, gentian root chips, mugwort, quassia bark chips, sarsaparilla root chips, and wormwood

CONVERSIONS

The recipes in this book were developed using standard U.S. measures following U.S. government guidelines. These charts offer equivalents for U.S. and metric measures. All conversions are approximate and have been rounded up or down to the nearest whole number.

Example

1 teaspoon = 4.9292 milliliters, rounded up to 5 milliliters

1 ounce = 28.3495 grams, rounded down to 28 grams

VOLUME CONVERSIONS

U.S.		Metric
-	1 teaspoon	5 milliliters
¼ ounce	1½ teaspoons	8 milliliters
-	2 teaspoons	10 milliliters
½ ounce	1 tablespoon	15 milliliters
¾ ounce	4½ teaspoons	23 milliliters
1 ounce	2 tablespoons	30 milliliters
2 ounces	¼ cup	59 milliliters
-	⅓ cup	79 milliliters
3 ounces	6 tablespoons	90 milliliters
4 ounces	½ cup	118 milliliters
6 ounces	¾ cup	177 milliliters
8 ounces	1 cup	237 milliliters
10 ounces	1¼ cups	296 milliliters
12 ounces	1½ cups	355 milliliters
16 ounces	2 cups (1 pint)	473 milliliters
20 ounces	2½ cups	591 milliliters
24 ounces	3 cups	710 milliliters
32 ounces	4 cups (1 quart)	0.946 liter

WEIGHT CONVERSIONS

ounces	grams
½	14
¾	21
1	28
1½	43
2	57
2½	71
3	85
3½	99
4	113
4½	128
5	142
6	170
7	198
8	227
9	255
10	283
12	340
16 (1 pound)	454

OVEN TEMPERATURES

Fahrenheit	Celsius	Gas Mark
225	105	¼
250	120	½
275	135	1
300	150	2
325	165	3
350	180	4
375	190	5
400	200	6
425	220	7
450	230	8
475	245	9

INDEX

Note: Page references in *italics* refer to photographs.